THE SUF
ESTUA

A REPORT BY THE SUFFOLK WILDLIFE TRUST ON THE WILDLIFE AND CONSERVATION OF THE SUFFOLK ESTUARIES

by C. H. Beardall
R. C. Dryden
T. J. Holzer

Published by the Suffolk Wildlife Trust

Funded by the Central Electricity Generating Board
through the World Wide Fund for Nature

ISBN 0 901588 01 6

Published by:
The Suffolk Wildlife Trust
Park Cottage,
Saxmundham,
Suffolk IP17 1DQ

1988

Contents

Chapter 4 The Future

Appendix

Further Reading

Acknowledgements

Many individuals and organisations have provided information for this report. Special thanks are due to the members of the Estuaries Project Steering Group, D. R. Moore (Suffolk Wildlife Trust), C. J. D. Shackles (Nature Conservancy Council), A. J. Prater (Royal Society for the Protection of Birds), M. T. Wright (British Trust for Ornithology) and J. T. Hindle (Suffolk County Council).

Our gratitude is also owed to the Institute of Terrestial Ecology, Anglian Water, Ministry for Agriculture, Food, and Fisheries, Universities of Essex and East Anglia, the Nature Conservancy Council, the multitude of volunteers who are involved in the Birds of Estuaries Enquiry and especially the estuary coordinators, and all others who have provided the data upon which this report is based.

We would also like to thank all the artists and photographers who have contributed to the report, acknowledgement is given alongside each plate and drawing.

Lastly we would like to thank the World Wide Fund for Nature and the Central Electricity Generating Board for supporting this Project.

Table 1. Physical features of the Suffolk Estuaries

	Length of tidal channel (km)	Area of saltmarsh (ha)	Area of mudflat (ha)	Area of river catchment (km2)
Blyth	10.0	55	276	214
Alde	10.5	91	346	
Ore	16.5	132	143	325
Butley	6.0	118	47	
Deben	18.5	251	447	408
Orwell	18.0	74	713	393
Stour	20.5	95	1506	896
Total		875	3478	2209

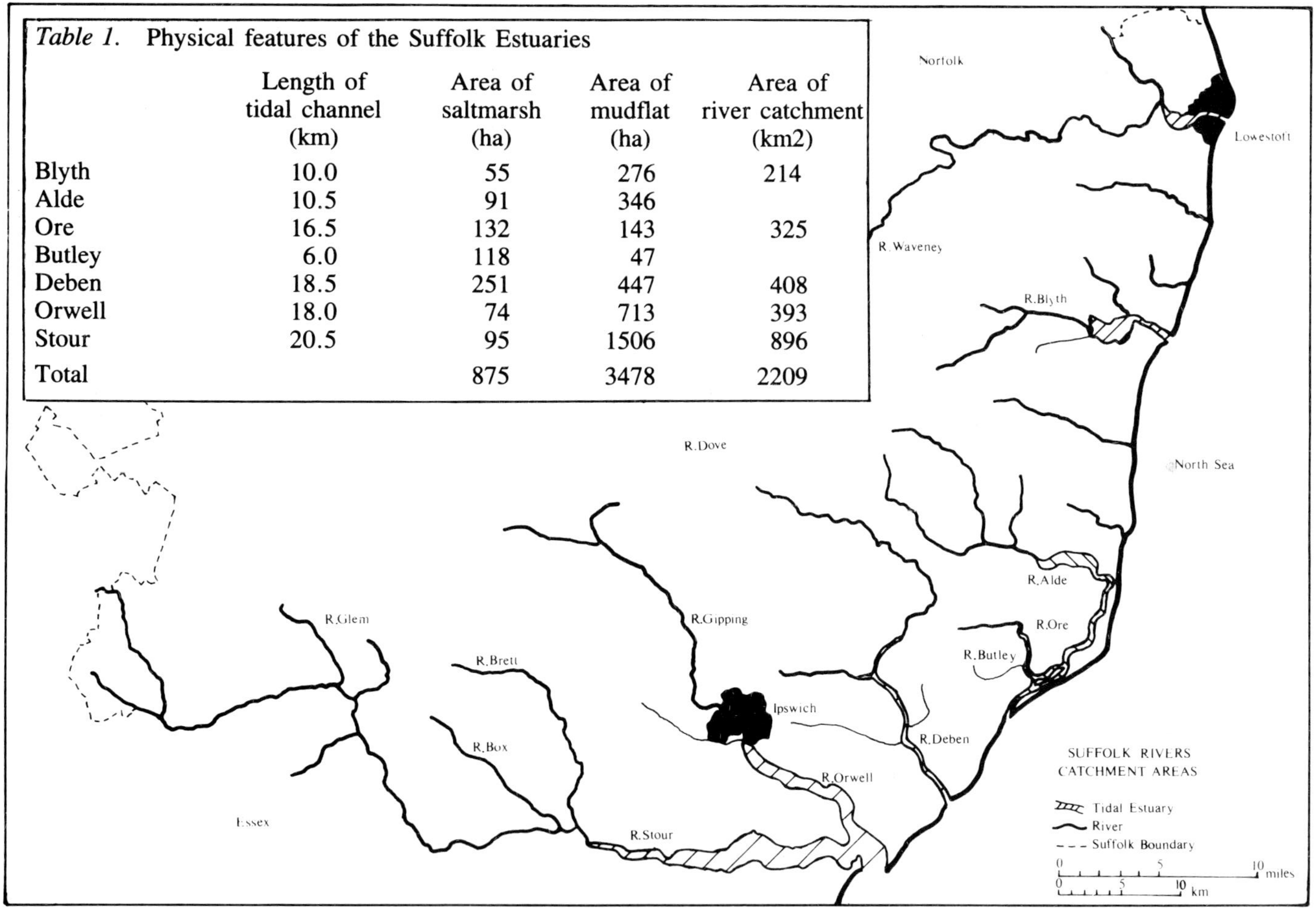

Figure 1. *The Suffolk estuaries and their river catchment areas.*

Chapter 1 Introduction

Suffolk Estuaries and the Suffolk Wildlife Trust

The coastal plain of Suffolk is dissected by five, long, meandering, shallow estuaries draining freshwater from the eastern region of Suffolk (figure 1). All five estuaries, the Stour*, Orwell, Deben, Alde/Ore/Butley complex, and Blyth, contain extensive areas of rich intertidal mudflat fringed by saltmarsh, and are of considerable natural interest.

The estuaries of Suffolk have for many centuries provided a valuable resource for the local inhabitants of the coastal region, providing an important source of food, salt and other natural products, as well as a means of communication and trade. The demands on our estuaries have, in the last century, increased dramatically in response to the needs of modern industry and transport, as well as recreational pursuits. Many activities, some traditional, some new, are now in conflict with the natural interest of our estuaries either individually or collectively.

In 1981 the Felixstowe Dock and Railway Company presented a Private Bill to Parliament, seeking permission to extend Felixstowe Dock over mudflats and saltmarsh at Fagbury on the Orwell estuary. The Suffolk Wildlife Trust's (SWT) opposition to the Bill, along with the Royal Society for the Protection of Birds (RSPB) and the Suffolk Ornithologists Group, highlighted the need for a more detailed understanding of the ecology of all our estuaries, to call upon should the threat of future developments arise elsewhere. In 1987 funding was gained through the World Wide Fund for Nature from the Central Electricity Generating Board, and the SWT Estuaries Project was initiated. The following chapters report

* The south bank of the Stour lies in Essex, but for the purpose of this report the whole estuary is considered as one unit.

the research of the Estuaries Project into the wildlife interest and conservation of the Suffolk estuaries.

The underlying aim of this report is to promote a better understanding of the Suffolk estuaries and all those activities that influence them. It is clearly the responsibility of all those using the estuaries to understand the wider implications of their actions, and that the requirements of commercial and recreational pursuits are carefully balanced with the needs of the estuarine ecosystem.

The introductory chapter describes the geological and human history of the estuaries, covering the past events that have influenced and created these areas as we know them today. The important physical and biological factors that influence life within an estuary are also briefly outlined.

The following section describes the wildlife interest of the Suffolk estuaries, highlighting particular aspects that are of regional, national, or international importance. Chapter three investigates the impact of all activities that may potentially influence estuarine wildlife, from bait-digging to channel dredging and dock activities.

Finally, the conflicts on our estuaries today are summarised and where possible proposals are put forward that may lessen the environmental impact of damaging activities and help secure their long term conservation. Areas requiring further research are identified and discussed.

All species names are written in English in the text (except where none is known or where confusion would arise) with the Latin nomenclature given in the appendix.

Geological History of the Suffolk Estuaries

In geological terms the majority of estuaries are recent in origin, having formed since the end of the last Ice Age ten thousand years ago. With the exception of the Ore, the Suffolk estuaries have been created by the drowning of river valleys with tidal water. In the last ice age Suffolk was covered by vast sheets of ice, and the British Isles were an integral part of the continental land mass. During this period the rivers of Suffolk were tributaries of the Thames, which flowed east before joining the Rhine in the middle of what is now the North Sea Basin. From there the combined river flowed north before entering the sea. As the glaciers melted, the sea level rose, flooding the continental shelf and drowning the last link between Britain and Europe.

Analysis of the intertidal mudflats of the Deben estuary reveal that it was approximately seven thousand years ago that the post-glacial rise in sea level, coupled with the subsidence of the North Sea Basin, flooded the river valleys of east Suffolk. The calm conditions that prevailed in the newly formed estuaries allowed sediment to settle, forming extensive areas of inter-tidal mudflat fringed by salt tolerant vegetation.

The Ore estuary has evolved more recently and by a different process. The deposition of a shingle spit (Orfordness) has deflected the course of the river Alde/Ore southwards, extending the estuary some 15 kilometres before entering the sea at North Weir Point. Shingle, consisting predominantly of flint derived both from the glacial erosion of chalk deposits and from coastal erosion, has over a period of time moved southwards down the coast of Suffolk, gradually extending Orford spit and forming the Ore estuary. This process, known as longshore drift, occurs as a result of waves striking the beach at an oblique southerly angle whilst the backwash returns perpendicular to the coastline, thus creating a movement of shingle southwards.

The progressive build-up of shingle on Orfordness, facilitating the accretion of mudflats and saltmarsh on the landward side, has been well documented and is estimated to have extended the spit some 12 metres a year over the last eight centuries. By the 12th century the ness had only developed as far as Orford, but after this period gradually extended further south, effectively severing the once prosperous port of Orford from the sea.

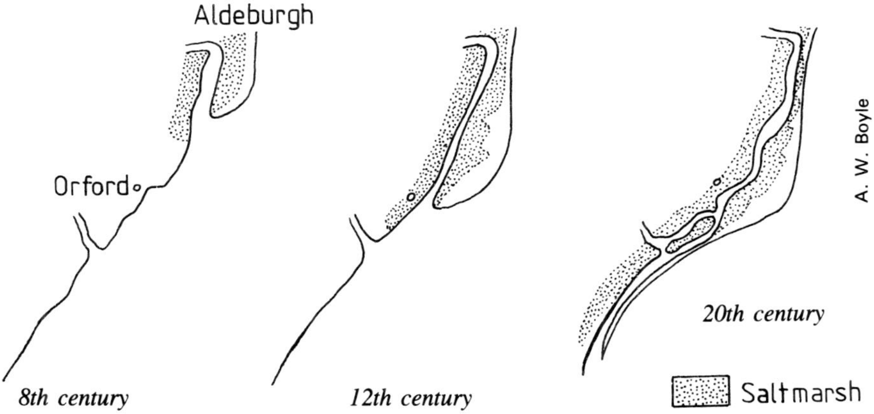

Historical maps of Suffolk in the 14th century indicate that the coastline was indented by many more coastal bays and estuaries than exist today (for instance the estuaries of the Minsmere, Dunwich, Hundred and Benacre rivers — see figure 2). The process of longshore drift has, however, sealed the mouth of these rivers

Figure 2. *Map of the Suffolk coastline in 1575 by Christopher Saxton. (Reproduced by kind permission of the Suffolk Records Office).*

with shingle bars, excluding tidal inundation and creating brackish lagoons.

The solid geology of the Suffolk coastal region has been influenced by the deposition of various marine sediments, whilst the land mass has progressed through cycles of marine submergence and subsequent exposure (figure 3). During the Mesozoic Era 500 metres of chalk were deposited, over which a variety of sediments were laid during the Tertiary period. London Clay formed the surface of the coastal plain in south east Suffolk and it is upon this that the rivers of the Stour, Orwell/Gipping and Deben originally ran. Subsequent submergence during warmer periods allowed further sediments to settle resulting in the formation of crags (consisting of shells and the remains of other marine organisms). Glacial materials, dominated by sand and gravels, have more recently been deposited in the eastern region of Suffolk on top of the underlying crags and clays.

The Tertiary rocks (London Clay and Coralline Crag) are rarely exposed at the land surface, except where the glacial deposits have been eroded by the passage of rivers. Evidence of these under-lying rocks can be seen in the Stour, Orwell and Deben estuaries where London Clay and Red Crag outcrop in localised areas. The underlying rock of the Mesozoic era is only exposed in the Orwell estuary where the central channel is dredged down to the chalk bed. North of the Deben the geology is dominated by crags of the Pleistocene period (predominantly Red Crag). However, the older Coralline Crag of the Pliocene era surfaces in a ridge between Orford and Aldeburgh through which the Alde estuary dissects its passage.

The intertidal mudflats have been derived from these underlying sedimentary deposits, as well as from the Boulder Clay that dominates much of the catchment area of the coastal rivers.

Human History of the Suffolk Estuaries

For thousands of years the Suffolk estuaries remained largely unaltered by human activities. As the demand for agricultural land escalated, the fertile intertidal zone of the low lying coastal plain became a prime area for reclamation. The earliest embankments in Britain probably date back to Roman times, although the main impetus was in the 11th to 13th centuries, and again in the 16th and 17th centuries.

Reclamation of the high marsh was achieved by direct enclosure with a sea wall, but methods were also used to promote the level of mudflat or saltmarsh prior to "inning". A process known as warping, the construction of a small earth wall or line of faggots, was used to reduce water turbulence and enhance the deposition of sediments. Once the levels of mudflat or saltmarsh had been raised, sea walls were constructed and the tide excluded. Whilst the reclamation of saltmarsh dates back to medieval times, enclosure of intertidal mudflats is perhaps a more recent trend. Once reclaimed and drained, alluvial sediment provided extremely fertile farmland.

Although some walls may date back to Roman times, the earliest evidence of "inning" in Suffolk is perhaps the construction of sea walls around Orford Castle in 1169. The majority of walls were, however, constructed in the 16th and 17th centuries. By 1842 the extent of reclamation on the Blyth estuary was such that approximately 1100 hectares of the intertidal zone had been converted to arable

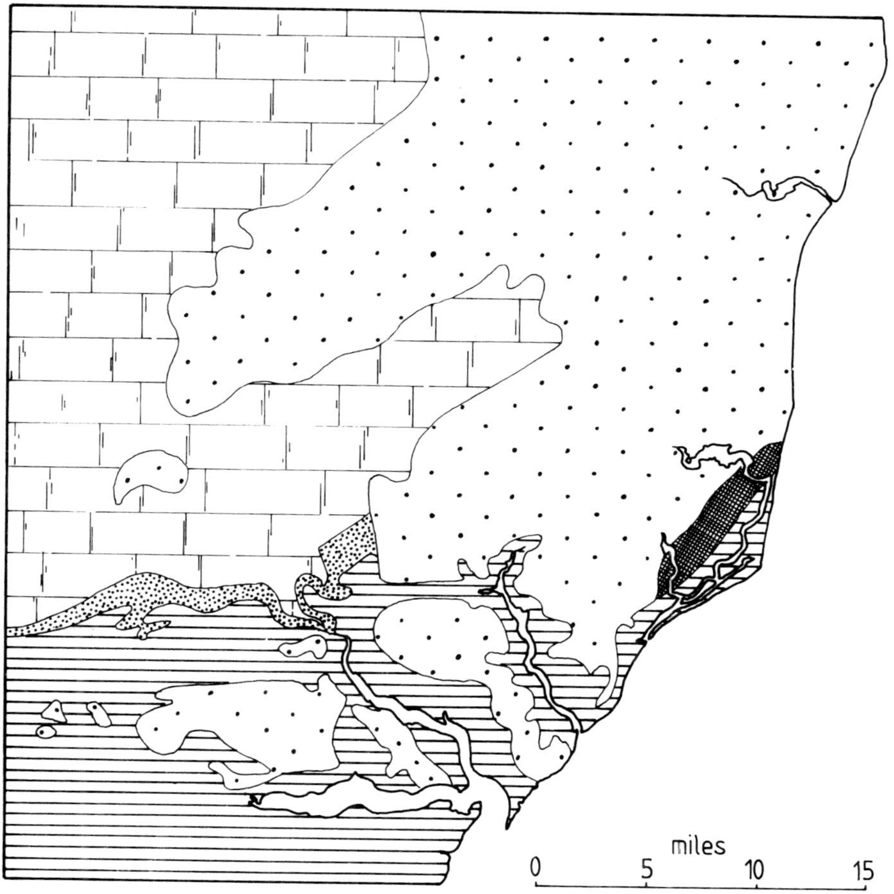

Pleistocene Crags	Pleistocene	- Quaternary era	2 million years ago
Coralline Crag	Pleiocene	Tertiary era	4 m.y.a.
London Clay	Eocene		15 m.y.a.
Reading and Thanet beds			
Chalk	Cretaceous	- Mesozoic era	70 - 130 m.y.a.

Figure 3. *The geology of the coastal region of Suffolk.*

land, restricting the estuary to a thin channel extending 10.0 kilometres inland to Blyford Bridge (see figure 4). Today, due to a series of breaches in the sea walls, 250 hectares have been returned to the intertidal zone (predominantly mudflat). One only has to consider the enormous area of Suffolk farmland protected

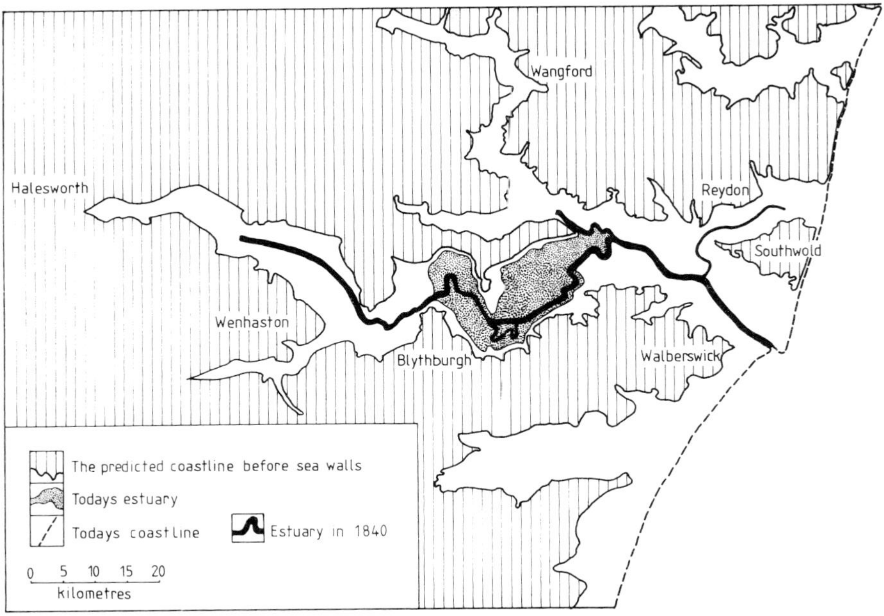

Figure 4. *Reclamation along the Blyth estuary, showing the probable coastline before the construction of sea walls, the extent of reclamation in 1840, and the estuary and coastline today.*

by sea walls to realise the extent of reclaimed saltmarsh and mudflat. This may amount to 10,800 hectares or 2.5 times the area of the total intertidal zone that remains today (summarised in table 2).

Table 2. Estimated areas of reclaimed saltmarsh and mudflat on the Suffolk Estuaries.

Estuary	Area reclaimed (hectares)
Blyth	1278
Alde	1450
Ore	2515
Butley	1004
Deben	2242
Orwell	983
Stour	1601
Total	10,817

The loss of estuarine habitat due to reclamation for agricultural land and flood protection has been reflected nationwide and it is estimated that of the area of saltmarsh that existed 500 years ago only 45% remains today. In Suffolk, as in many other regions of Britain, reclamation for agricultural land has ceased. The 20th century has, however, brought new pressures to the intertidal zone, demanding land for industry, tidal barrage schemes, marinas, ports, and the tipping of refuse and fly-ash. All three of the major ports on the Suffolk estuaries, Felixstowe, Harwich, and Ipswich, are either in the process of infilling mudflat and saltmarsh or have obtained the necessary permission to do so (see chapter 3).

The Suffolk estuaries have been subjected to many other activities that have influenced their ecology. The Orwell has been used for navigation to Ipswich since Roman times, and throughout the centuries the Port of Ipswich has been one of the most prosperous in Britain. The ecological consequences of port-related activities are covered in detail in chapter 3. Trade and shipping have also influenced the history of the Stour, Deben, and to a lesser extent the Alde, Ore, Butley and Blyth. Although many activities in the past will have had little impact on our estuaries, the last few decades have seen an ever increasing demand for a wide variety of water based leisure pursuits, commercial operations, and the discharge of industrial and domestic effluents. These varied impacts have created many ecological changes that may conflict with the long term conservation of the Suffolk estuaries.

Physical Characteristics of Estuaries

An estuary can be defined as a semi-enclosed area at the mouth of a river, where freshwater drained from the land is mixed, to some degree, with saltwater brought in from the sea. The four crucial physical features that collectively make estuaries unique amongst aquatic ecosystems are a gradient of salinity, relatively sheltered conditions which allow sedimentation, the influence of the tides, and a regular input of nutrients.

SALINITY

The mixing of salt and freshwater within an estuary creates a salinity gradient between the head and mouth. The salinity gradient is not static and fluctuates twice-daily with the tides, as well as seasonally in relation to the input of freshwater into the estuary. During times of rain, dilution by fresh water pushes the salinity gradient seawards, whilst during the summer seawater is less diluted, and able to penetrate further up the estuary (see figure 5). The freshwater input into the Suffolk estuaries is normally a small percentage of the total tidal volume (average of 0.46% for the Orwell estuary) and hence high salinity is maintained well towards the head of the estuaries (figure 6).

In addition to the salinity gradient along an estuary, there is also a vertical gradient in the water column, created by the differing densities of fresh and salt water. Where an estuary has a large input of freshwater, layering may occur in which the less dense freshwater floats above saltwater to create an underlying salt-wedge. This situation may only occur in the upper reaches of the Suffolk estuaries during winter flood periods, when the freshwater input is at its highest. Under normal conditions however our estuaries are well mixed with little variation

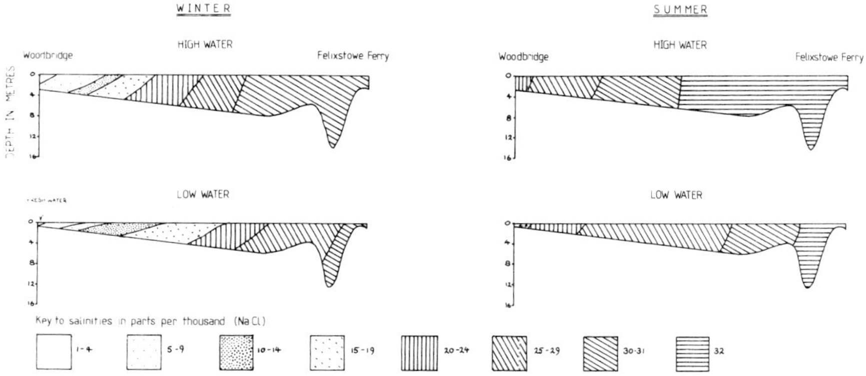

Figure 5. *Salinity gradients along the Deben estuary during high and low water, in both the summer and winter.*

in salinity from the top to the bottom of the water column (see figure 5).

Fluctuating salinity gradients create serious physiological problems for sedentary animals living within estuaries and affect both the distribution and abundance of organisms that are able to colonise this harsh environment (see chapter 2).

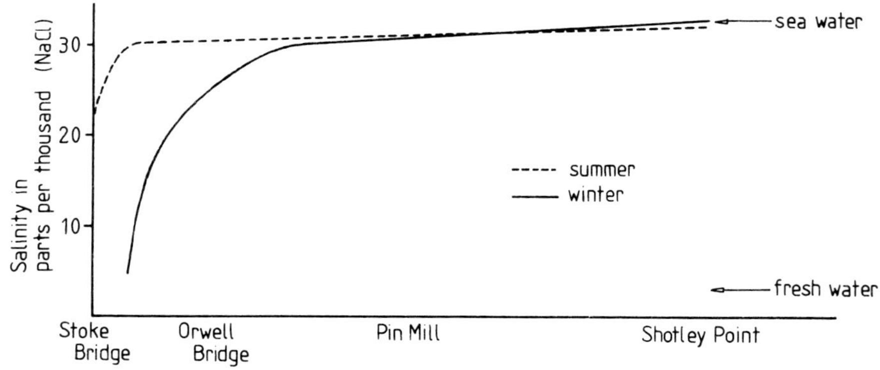

Figure 6. *Surface water salinity gradient along the Orwell estuary during the summer and winter.*

SEDIMENTATION

Estuaries are typically semi-enclosed and as such are relatively sheltered from the action of wind and waves. The calm conditions that prevail allow suspended sediment, derived both from the sea and the freshwater catchment area, to settle, forming extensive areas of intertidal mudflats. The patterns of sedimentation along an estuary vary according to the relative influence of the tide, wind, waves and river currents (see chapter 2), leading to the deposition of finer sediment in the inner sheltered reaches.

The origin of sediment varies between estuaries but in Suffolk studies on the Orwell and Deben have shown that today the dominant source is from the sea. In the Deben, for instance, the annual input of sediment from the sea is sixteen times greater than that from the river.

THE INFLUENCE OF TIDES

The third major characteristic of an estuary is the influence of twice-daily tides. Britain experiences a relatively large tidal range that varies according to location. The Bristol Channel, for instance, has an average tidal range of 9.4 metres (maximum of 12 metres), whilst in Suffolk the mean tidal range is approximately 2.9 metres (maximum of 4.3 metres). Imposed on a twice-daily tidal cycle is also a fortnightly and six-monthly cycle such that spring tides occur every two weeks and with a much greater range every six months. Regional variations also occur depending on the physical characteristics of the estuary and weather conditions. For example, severe northerly storms in the North Sea pushing water south, can cause tide heights on the south east coast that may exceed by 2 metres those predicted from astronomical events. The tidal range within an estuary may also be influenced by constricted water flow through the mouth, resulting in a reduced range in the inner reaches.

The exposure of intertidal mudflats at low tide causes large temperature fluctuations within the surface of the sediment. Mudflat temperatures reach their maximum during summer day-time low tides, whilst in winter extremely cold nights can cause freezing, resulting in the death of many mud-dwelling invertebrates.

THE INFLUENCE OF NUTRIENTS

In contrast to other ecosystems, estuaries are supplied with a twice daily input of fresh nutrients derived from the freshwater catchment area, the sea and the fringing habitats. As a result intertidal areas are one of the most productive on earth and can be up to eight times more prolific than a comparable area of arable land and twenty times more productive than the open sea.

Wildlife and Habitat Protection on the Suffolk Estuaries

As a result of the rich ecological interest of the Suffolk estuaries (described in chapter 2), many areas are afforded regional, national and/or international protection through a variety of designations (see figure 7). Nature conservation designations help to promote sympathetic management and public awareness, control developments and damaging operations, and provide a national and international context to assess the importance of a specific site.

NATIONAL PROTECTION

The Nature Conservancy Council (NCC) has power under the Wildlife and Countryside Act 1981 and 1985 (and previously the National Parks and Access to the Countryside Act 1949) to designate areas of outstanding national importance for their wildlife or geological interest as Sites of Special Scientific Interest (SSSI). The owner/occupier of a SSSI is required to notify the NCC if they are intending to carry out any potentially damaging operation in order to allow the NCC to

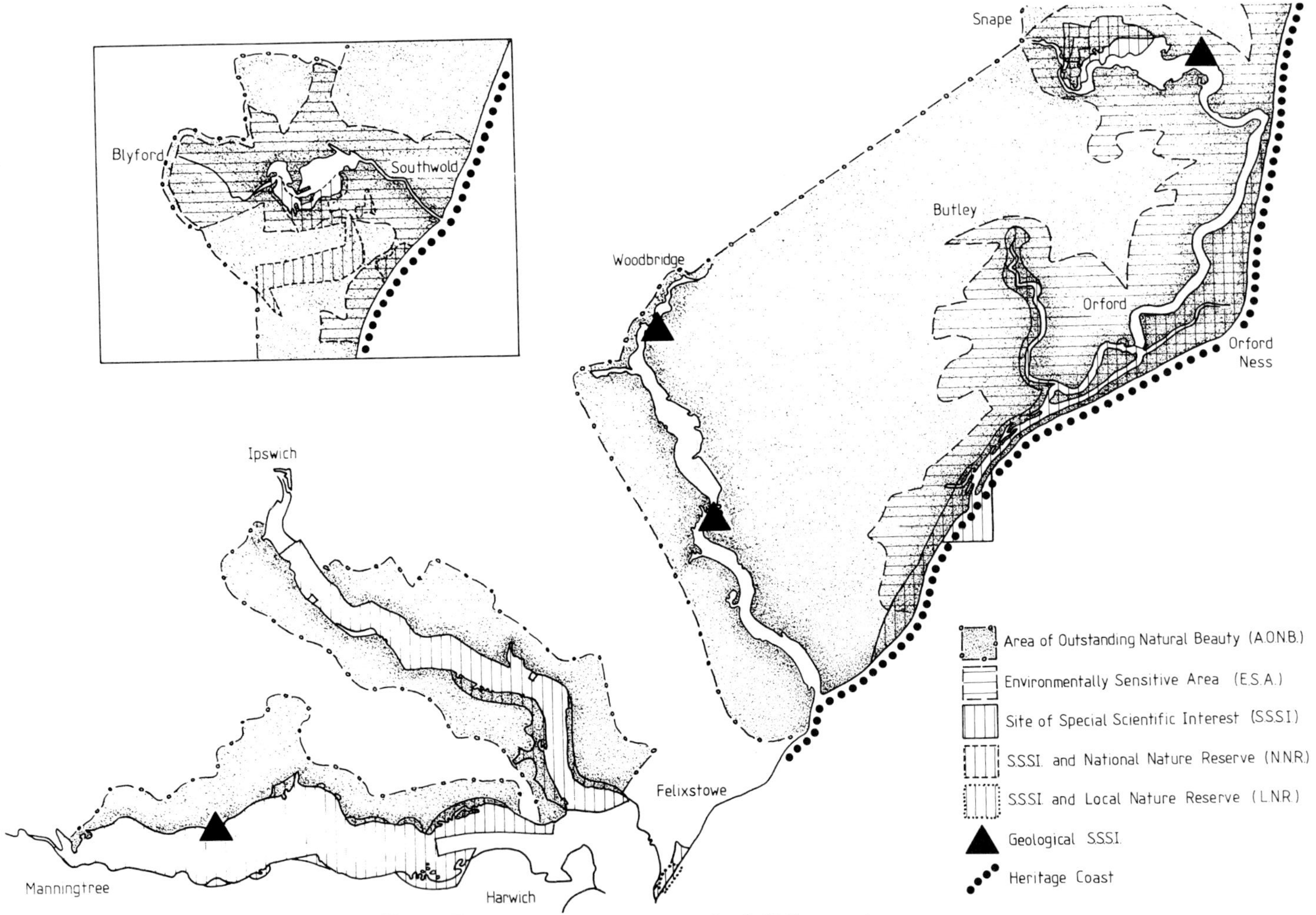

Figure 7. *Designations protecting the Suffolk estuaries.*

offer management advice or enter into a voluntary management agreement. The NCC may offer financial compensation for profits lost, if the owner agrees to forgo a proposed operation considered by the NCC to be damaging. If Local Authorities receive a planning application for any development on a SSSI then they are required to consult the NCC, however once consultation is complete the normal planning processes apply.

Both the Stour and Orwell estuaries have been designated as SSSI's, primarily on ornithological grounds, providing over-wintering feeding areas for nationally and internationally significant populations of waders and wildfowl. The Stour also contains important geological exposures at Stutton and Wrabness. Landguard, a sand and shingle spit protecting the haven ports of Felixstowe and Harwich, was designated in 1973 for its botanical interest. To a lesser extent it is an important landfall site for migrating birds and a breeding site for little terns. Landguard has also been designated as a Local Nature Reserve by the Suffolk County Council, and is therefore subject to specific by-laws that further promote the protection and management of the area. The Deben estuary contains two small SSSI's, both designated for their geological interest. Ramsholt cliff is of interest for a number of different outcrops including Coralline Crag, Coprolite, and Boxstone. Ferry Cliff, Sutton, is of interest for mammalian fossils.

The Orfordness-Havergate SSSI, which includes Butley Creek and part of the Ore estuary, was designated for the following reasons. The shingle structures of Orfordness and Shingle Street are of great physiographic importance whilst the cliff at Gedgrave is of geological significance. The mudflats, saltmarshes, vegetated shingle and coastal lagoons are botanically and ornithologically important. Havergate Island and the south section of Orfordness have also been designated as a National Nature Reserve managed by the RSPB and NCC respectively. Further up the estuary, in the inner Alde, there are two SSSI's. The area of intertidal mudflat adjacent to Snape Warren on the north bank is part of the Snape Warren and Blackheath Wood SSSI and an outcrop of Coralline Crag at Round Hill Pit has been designated for its geological interest. Lastly, the south bank of the Blyth forms part of the Walberswick National Nature Reserve and provides a mosaic of important habitats.

On a regional basis the majority of Suffolk estuaries are also given special protection through the designation of the Suffolk Coast and Heaths Area of Outstanding Natural Beauty and Suffolk Heritage Coast. Both designations, made by the Countryside Commission and implemented by the County Council, promote a positive and planned management of the coastal area, safeguarding the landscape and wildlife interest, whilst providing for recreational activities and sympathetic developments.

INTERNATIONAL PROTECTION

In 1973 the United Kingdom signed the RAMSAR convention to promote the conservation of internationally important wetland sites. Under this agreement Minsmere and the Walberswick marshes have been designated as RAMSAR sites, whilst the Stour, Orwell, Havergate Island and Orfordness, all of which fulfil the criteria, await designation. Further international protection is afforded to these sites under the European Community Directive on the Conservation of Wild Birds. Under this agreement, signed by the UK in 1979, sites of specific importance for rare birds or "regularly occurring migratory species" are to be designated as Special Protection Areas (SPA) in which strict planning controls will be enforced. Even though none of the Suffolk estuaries have been formally designated as SPA's, from December 1987 all proposed SPA's, which include the Stour and Orwell estuaries, Orfordness and Havergate Island, Minsmere and the Walberswick Marshes, are, in the eyes of the planning authorities, to be considered as designated.

Chapter 2 Wildlife of the Suffolk Estuaries

Introduction

The five estuaries of Suffolk support a particularly rich assemblage of plants and animals. Much of this interest is not evident until examined in detail and within the context of the whole estuarine ecosystem.

This chapter reviews the wildlife interest of the Suffolk estuaries. Emphasis is given to mudflats and saltmarsh, although the important adjacent habitats of shingle and grazing marsh are also covered. The ecology of each habitat is briefly outlined, followed by sections on the flora and fauna.

Mudflats

Ecology of Mudflats

PHYSICAL CHARACTERISTICS

Intertidal mudflats are created by the deposition of both inorganic and organic sediment. These are derived from either terrestrial or marine erosion, and transported into the estuary with the tides or river flow.

The deposition of suspended sediment is influenced by the energy of water movements created by tides, wind, waves and river currents. At the mouth of an estuary strong tidal currents and wave action keeps sediment suspended in the water column. Only heavy particles can settle, forming intertidal flats dominated by sand and shingle. In the more sheltered inner reaches, fine particles of silt and clay settle to form the characteristic mudflats of the intertidal zone. Towards the head of an estuary finer particles are kept in suspension by the influence of river currents, whereas larger sediment may settle. The mixing of salt and fresh water also causes clay particles to adhere to each other, thus forming heavier sediment capable of settling in faster currents. There is therefore a characteristic gradation of particle size found within an estuary, from larger sediment at the mouth and head, to increasingly finer muds and silt in the inner, more sheltered reaches.

Estuarine mudflats are in a constant state of flux, not only with the tides and seasons but also on a geological time scale. Many habitats within an estuary are essentially short-lived, the gradual process of silting promoting natural succession from intertidal mudflats to tidal saltmarsh and eventually to dry land. Seasonal fluctuations in the height of mudflats may be substantial. Studies on the Deben have reported that during the spring and summer a mudflat accretion of some five centimetres can occur, whilst during the winter, the same amount can be lost through erosion. During the summer, vegetation (algae and eel-grass) growing on the surface of the mudflats and the mucus secreted by mud-dwelling microscopic algae, help trap and bind the sediment and reduce tidal scour. In the winter when plant material is absent, wave action and tidal scour cause erosion. The formation of small blocks of ice in severe winters, may also promote erosion of mudflat and saltmarsh by scouring the mud surface.

Eel-grass at Nacton on the River Orwell.

Rapid changes in salinity, temperature and turbidity, caused by the twice-daily cycle of the tides, collectively create a demanding habitat for estuarine life and to a large extent dictate the species that can colonise this ecosystem. As a result intertidal mudflats tend to support fewer species than are found in the adjacent sea or freshwater environments. However, many of the species that are able to colonise estuaries occur at exceedingly high population densities, reflecting the abundance of food and lack of competition.

THE INFLUENCE OF SALINITY ON ESTUARINE ORGANISMS

Mud-dwelling organisms adopt various strategies to overcome the problems of fluctuating salinity. Most marine species are able to regulate body fluids as the external water conditions change. Other species have a higher tolerance and allow their body fluids to change with the external salinity.

Some organisms avoid the worst rigours of salinity changes by burrowing into the sediment where the salinity is relatively stable. In doing this they also avoid dehydration and extreme temperatures. Others are able to migrate or, in the case of bivalves (e.g. cockle), close their shells when the salinity becomes intolerable. The distribuion of estuarine organisms is, however, restricted to those areas of the estuary that lie within the salinity tolerance limits of each species.

THE INFLUENCE OF SUBSTRATE ON ESTUARINE ORGANISMS

Substrate characteristics also have a strong influence on the distribution and abundance of estuarine organisms. As the particle size of sediment decreases the organic content increases, providing more food for detritus-feeding invertebrates.

However, fine silt interferes with respiratory and feeding organs, limiting the substrates different invertebrates can inhabit. In addition, fine substrates are also rendered unsuitable by the lack of oxygen and presence of waste compounds, such as ammonia, methane and hydrogen sulphide, created by bacterial decomposion of organic matter.

THE ESTUARINE FOOD CHAIN

Primary production within an estuary comes largely from microscopic algae within the sediment, plant communities inhabiting saltmarsh and mudflats, and to a lesser degree microscopic drifting plants (phytoplankton). In contrast to terrestial ecosystems, there are few herbivores and much of the primary production is circulated within the estuary as detritus (organic debris from decomposing plants). The constant input of detritus, derived principally from the sea but also from the river catchment area and the fringing habitats, provides the major resource fuelling the estuarine ecosystem. It is this detritus that supports the enormous populations of both deposit and suspension feeders inhabiting the intertidal mudflats. In the Suffolk estuaries these communities are dominated by molluscs (e.g. mussels, cockles, tellins, gapers and the mud snail *Hydrobia ulvae*), crustacea (e.g. the shrimp-like *Corophium volutator*) and polychaete worms (e.g. lugworm). These species are in turn consumed by a variety of predators, including invertebrates (e.g. ragworm) and various species of birds and fish.

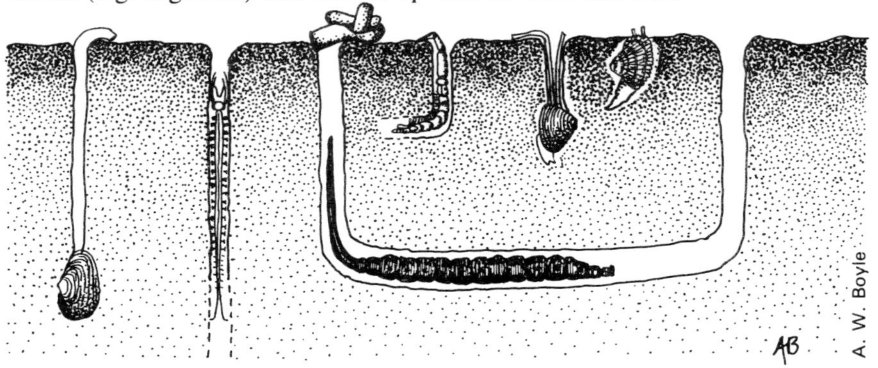

Mud-dwelling invertebrates:— sand gaper, ragworm, lugworm, Corophium volutator, tellin and cockle.

The distribution of waders and wildfowl feeding on intertidal mudflats is to a large extent dictated by the distribution of the prey species. The feeding methods of each bird are adapted to specific groups of prey items. Long billed waders (e.g. curlew) feed by probing for the deeper burrowing invertebrates (e.g. lugworm) whilst species with short bills (e.g. ringed plover), feeding by sight, predate invertebrates on the mud surface. In addition some wildfowl feed upon algae (predominantly *Enteromorpha*) and eel-grass growing on the mudflat.

Estuaries are also used by large numbers of fish as both feeding and nursery grounds. In some estuaries fish may even be the major predators of bottom-living invertebrates. For instance, research on the Ythan estuary in Scotland has shown that the amount of invertebrate biomass consumed by fish is three times that taken by waders and wildfowl. Some species of fish (e.g. sand goby and flounder) spend most of their life within an estuary, only returning to sea to spawn, and can be considered as estuarine species. Others (salmon, sea trout and eel) merely pass through or spend a particular stage of their life within an estuary (e.g. herring and sprat). Species which are known to frequent the intertidal zone in Suffolk include the common eel, salmon and sea trout, pipefish, bass, grey mullet, cod, whiting, flounders, sole, plaice, rockling, guppy, and herring. Some of these species have in the past provided important fisheries for the local population and are still occasionally trawled.

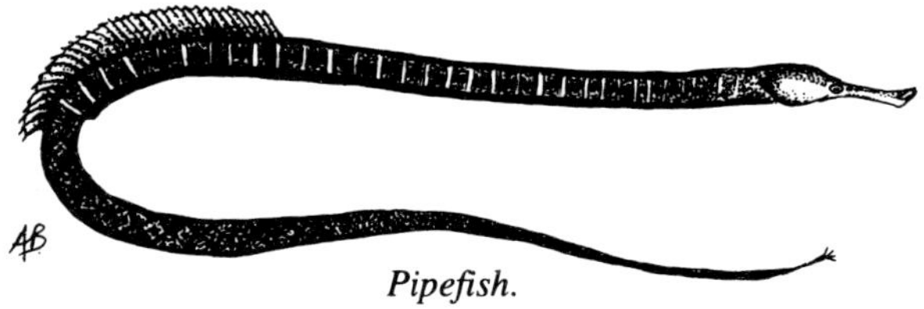

Pipefish.

A. W. Boyle

Mud-dwelling Invertebrates

Few studies have investigated the invertebrate fauna of the intertidal mudflats in Suffolk. In 1973 the Institute of Terrestial Ecology (ITE) carried out a study of the Thames estuary complex (covering fourteen estuaries in Kent, Essex and Suffolk, including the Stour and Orwell) in order to assess the environmental impact of the proposed airport at Maplin Sands (Foulness). This project included the first detailed study of the invertebrate fauna of the Stour and Orwell estuaries. The Suffolk Wildlife Trust has since completed two similar studies on the Orwell (1984 and 1986) in connection with the Felixstowe Dock and Railway Bill (see chapter 3). Anglian Water (Colchester Division) have also repeated the ITE study on the Stour (1985), whilst the Norwich Division has monitored the Orwell (1984). To date there have been no studies on the invertebrate fauna of the Deben, Alde/Ore/Butley or Blyth.

All the above surveys recorded a high diversity of species in both the Stour and Orwell and the ITE study found the Orwell to have the highest diversity of any estuary in south-east England. It was suggested that this may be connected with the wide variety of substrates found within this estuary. Of the fourteen estuaries analysed the Orwell and Stour were also the most productive in terms of biomass of invertebrates per square metre of mudflat.

A comparison of the ITE study and that of the SWT in 1986 indicates some interesting changes in the distribution and abundance of invertebrate populations inhabiting the Orwell mudflats (see table 3). It is apparent that there has been a reduction in the occurrence of molluscs, and in particular the common cockle, baltic tellin, and the mud gastropod *Hydrobia ulvae*. The latter represented 48.5% of the specimens collected in 1973 but only 9% of those collected in 1986. By contrast the ragworm and the amphipod, *Corophium volutator*, have increased dramatically, the former species occurring in 51% of the samples in 1973 and 87% of the samples in 1986. During this same period the average productivity per square metre of mudflat would appear to have decreased.

Table 3 The percentage occurrence of selected species of invertebrates in sediment samples from the Orwell and Stour. Data taken from studies by ITE (1973) and SWT (1986) for the Orwell and ITE (1973) and AW (1985) for the Stour.

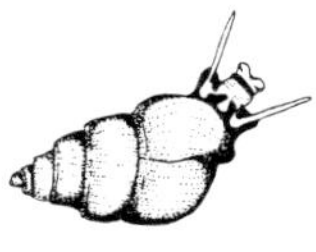

Hydrobia ulvae.

	Orwell		Stour	
	1973	1986	1973	1985
ANNELLIDS				
Ragworm	51%	87%	41%	63%
MOLLUSCS				
Common Cockle	82%	48%	83%	46%
Baltic Tellin	89%	34%	94%	87%
Hydrobia ulvae	92%	59%	96%	52%
ANTHROPDS				
Corophium volutator	15%	29%	16%	51%

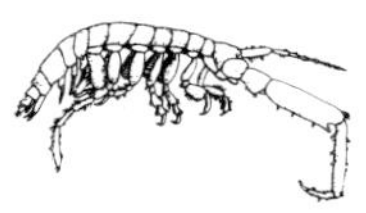

Corophium volutator.

On average each square metre of mudflat on the Orwell contained 0.6 kilograms of invertebrates in 1986, and in certain areas this figure was even as high as 2.0 kilograms per square metre. Ragworm were recorded at densities of up to 10,000 per square metre.

Figure 8 compares the profile of productivity along the Orwell for 1973 and 1986. It is interesting to note that during this period the upper reaches of the estuary have become more productive, whilst the lower reaches, particularly on the south shore, have become less productive. The increase in sewage effluent discharged at Cliff Quay (15% over the last fifteen years) could possibly account for the increased productivity in the upper reaches of the estuary. Figure 9 demonstrates the colonisation of the upper reaches by ragworm since 1973, especially in the mudflats adjacent to the Cliff Quay sewage outfall. It is harder to understand the decrease in productivity in the lower reaches, however these mudflats do appear to be subject to severe erosion which may inhibit the existence of sustainable populations of invertebrates.

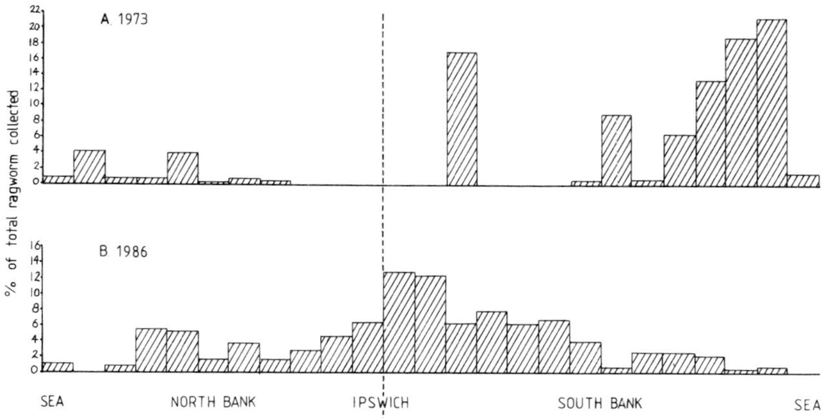

Figure 9. *Changes in the distribution of ragworm along the intertidal mudflats of the Orwell, between 1973 (histogram A, taken from ITE unpublished data) and 1986 (histogram B, SWT study).*

Many of the changes in the invertebrate populations of the Orwell appear also to have occurred on the Stour. For instance molluscs (predominantly baltic tellin,

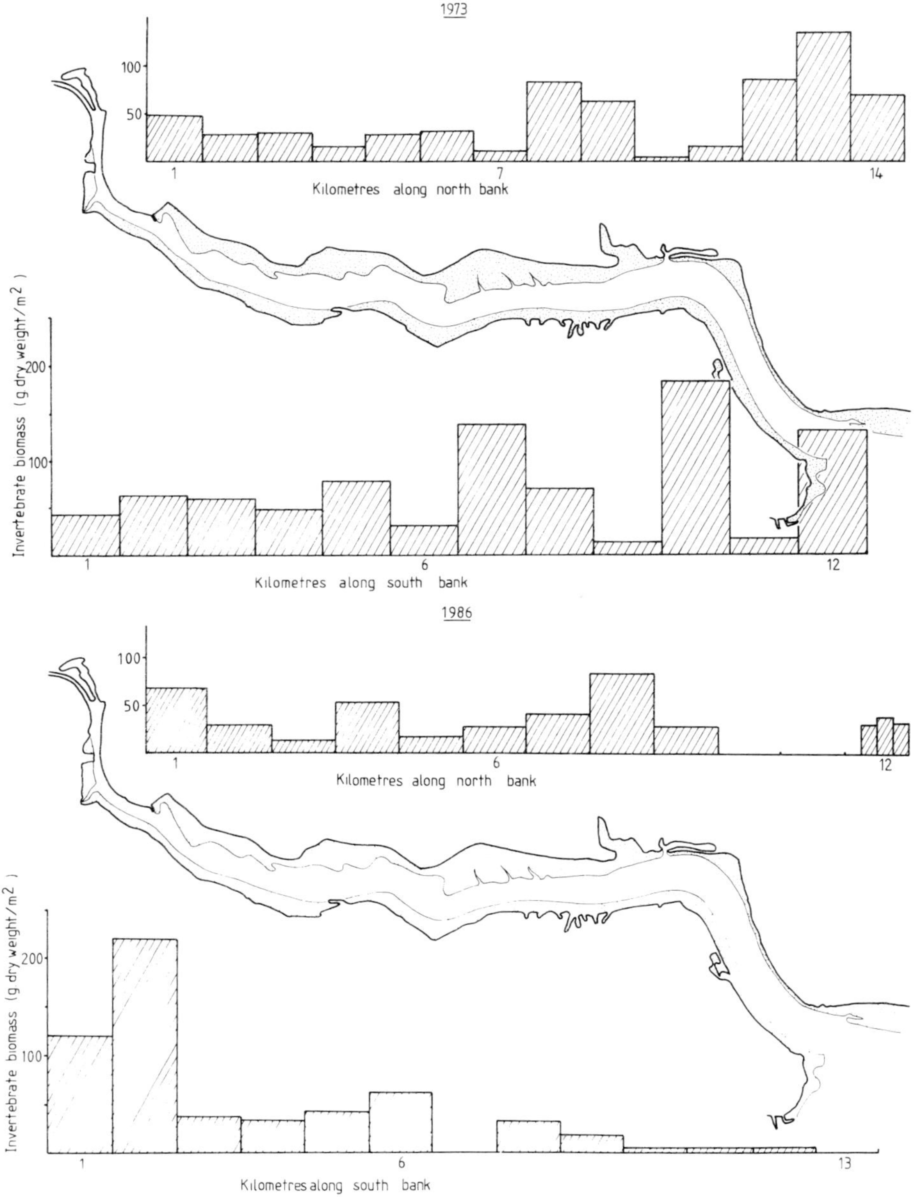

Figure 8. *Profile of the biomass of invertebrates (in grams dry weight per square metre) inhabiting the intertidal mudflats of the Orwell estuary. A comparison between 1973 (top histogram, taken from ITE unpublished data) and 1986 (lower histogram, SWT study).*

C. H. Beardall

Plate 1. *Reclaimed marsh on the Deben.*

Suffolk Underwater Studies, Orford

Plate 2. *The mouth of the Deben estuary.*

R. C. Dryden/D. R. Moore

Plate 3. *Intertidal mudflats on the Blyth estuary with (inset) a selection of mud-dwelling invertebrates.*

C. H. Beardall

Plate 4. *Saltmarsh with salt pans, Butley Creek.*

P. G. Lawson

Sea aster.

R. C. Dryden

Plate 5. *Pioneer saltmarsh plants (glasswort and cord-grass) colonizing the edge of a saltmarsh creek. Levington Creek. River Orwell.*

C. H. Beardall.

Plate 6. *Landguard Local Nature Reserve.*

C. H. Beardall

Plate 7. *Yellow-horned Poppy.*

R. C. Dryden

Plate 8. *Sea Pea.*

common cockle, *Hydrobia ulvae* and *Abra tenuis*) accounted for 90% of the specimens collected in 1973 by the ITE, but only 10% in the AW study (1985). Whilst the baltic tellin does not appear to have declined, the common cockle decreased from occurring in 83% of the samples in 1973 to only 46% in 1985, the exact decrease experienced on the Orwell. During this period there was also a substantial increase in the populations of segmented worms, which accounted for 9% of the individuals collected in 1973 and 70% in 1985.

In summary, on both the Orwell and the Stour there would appear to have been a simultaneous change in the invertebrate fauna from one dominated by molluscs in 1973, to the dominance of the segmented worms in 1985-7. The exact reasons for such a change are unclear, but may reflect natural population fluctuations or changing environmental conditions.

Waders and Wildfowl

The most conspicuous indication of the biological productivity of intertidal mudflats is the spectacular flocks of waders and wildfowl that characterise our estuaries during the winter months. The estuaries around Britain contain 2600 square kilometres of intertidal mudflat, providing feeding grounds for approximately one million waders, 40% of the total population wintering in Western Europe. Many more birds use our estuaries as refuelling stations whilst on migration between Arctic breeding grounds and wintering areas in Africa and southern Europe. The total number of wildfowl over-wintering in Britain is in excess of one million, although the number feeding on intertidal mudflat varies with the severity of the winter.

The importance of British estuaries for waders and wildfowl can be attributed to our relatively mild climate and large tidal range resulting in extensive areas of highly productive intertidal mudflats that rarely freeze, thus providing vital feeding grounds throughout the winter. Due to the reliance of the estuarine ecosystem on detritus and the heat storage capacity of the sea the biomass of invertebrates within the intertidal mudflats peaks in autumn, coinciding approximately with the maximum number of feeding waders.

To assess the conservation value of an estuary for each species of wader or wildfowl the 5th International Convention on the Conservation of Wetlands and Waterfowl (1974) proposed a set of criteria for identifying sites of national and international importance. A site is considered of international importance if it regularly holds 1% of the total population of a particular species found in a discrete geographical population. The waders and wildfowl in Britain belong to the over-wintering Western European populations. Similarly, a site that regularly holds 1% of the total national population of a specific species is considered to be of national importance. A site also qualifies as internationally important if it regularly holds more than 20,000 waterfowl.

The wader and wildfowl populations over-wintering on some of the Suffolk estuaries have been counted for many years as part of the national Birds of Estuaries Enquiry (BOEE), organised jointly by the British Trust for Ornithology (BTO), the Wildfowl Trust, the NCC and the RSPB. Complete coverage of all the Suffolk estuaries has only been achieved since 1985/6. The BOEE provides

Table 5. Waders and Wildfowl over-wintering on the Suffolk Estuaries. Numbers represent the mean of the number of birds counted during the mid-winter period (November to March), averaged over the last three years (1985-1988). (★ = less than one)

	Stour	Orwell	Deben	Alde/Ore/ Butley	Blyth
Black-Throated Diver	0	★	0	0	0
Great Northern Diver	★	0	0	0	0
Little Grebe	★	10	23	2	★
Great Crested Grebe	33	22	6	★	★
Red-Necked Grebe	0	★	0	★	0
Slavonian Grebe	0	★	0	0	0
Cormorant	107	129	56	61	9
Grey Heron	13	4	5	22	5
Mute Swan	208	48	89	137	8
Bewick's Swan	0	0	2	30	0
Whooper Swan	0	0	1	1	★
Bean Goose	0	0	0	1	0
White-Fronted Goose	0	★	9	46	0
Greylag Goose	0	1	1	1	1
Canada Goose	99	32	175	236	14
Barnacle Goose	★	★	★	★	★
Brent Goose	1126	779	838	296	2
Red-Breasted Goose	0	0	0	★	0
Shelduck	1056	610	828	686	309
Wigeon	1693	555	1177	3961	607
Gadwall	★	0	2	5	1
Teal	306	50	244	641	37
Mallard	1343	561	374	1032	93
Pintail	138	114	148	110	1
Shoveler	5	1	2	31	1
Pochard	5	25	3	14	1
Tufted Duck	1	56	28	47	0
Scaup	3	6	★	0	0
Eider	★	★	0	1	★
Long-Tailed Duck	0	1	0	0	0
Common Scoter	0	0	★	1	0
Velvet Scoter	0	0	0	★	0
Goldeneye	33	68	65	14	★
Smew	0	★	★	★	0
Red-Breasted Merganser	2	16	1	1	0
Goosander	0	0	★	★	0
Oystercatcher	554	983	128	50	30
Avocet	0	0	1	232	★
Ringed Plover	227	281	36	45	15
Golden Plover	11	47	70	167	★
Grey Plover	1002	180	81	79	17
Lapwing	927	859	888	2962	155
Knot	578	593	1	3	1
Sanderling	1	5	0	0	0
Dunlin	12485	5958	1225	1534	760
Ruff	0	0	0	1	0
Jack Snipe	0	1	★	★	0
Snipe	30	70	36	64	1
Black-Tailed Godwit	694	15	36	1	0
Bar-Tailed Godwit	★	1	1	6	★
Whimbrel	0	0	0	1	0
Curlew	642	389	275	633	21
Spotted Redshank	★	0	0	★	0
Redshank	1019	1034	930	649	381
Greenshank	★	0	★	★	0
Green Sandpiper	★	1	★	1	0
Common Sandpiper	0	★	★	0	0
Turnstone	356	240	7	9	★
Black-Headed Gull	1641	1727	501	1198	212
Common Gull	129	119	20	81	8
Lesser Black-Backed Gull	12	1	4	122	5
Herring Gull	44	53	101	1441	17
Glaucous Gull	0	0	★	★	0
Great Black-Backed Gull	57	27	20	256	13

yearly information on birds feeding on British estuaries and enables an accurate assessment of the importance of each estuary both in a national and international context.

The BOEE has identified a number of important populations of waders and wildfowl on the Suffolk estuaries (see table 4). In particular the Suffolk estuaries

Table 4. Waders and Wilfowl of national and international importance on the Suffolk Estuaries. N denotes nationally significant numbers, I denotes internationally significant numbers. Data taken from 1985-1988, using the average of the mid-winter peak counts for each species.

	Stour	Orwell	Deben	Alde/Ore/ Butley
Mute Swan	N			
Bewick's Swan				N
White-fronted Goose				N
Dark-bellied Brent Goose	I	I	I	
Shelduck	I	I	N	N
Wigeon	N		N	I
Pintail				N
Avocet				I
Ringed Plover	N	I		
Grey Plover	I	N		
Dunlin	N	N		
Black-tailed Godwit	I		N	
Redshank	I	N	N	N
Turnstone	N			

are internationally important for redshank, shelduck, ringed plover, grey plover, avocet and black-tailed godwit. Of special note is the Stour which holds the second largest population of over-wintering black-tailed godwits in Britain and the Butley/ Ore which is the only site in Britain to be of international importance for avocets.

During the winter of 1986/87 almost 45,000 birds over-wintered on the Suffolk estuaries, accounting for approximately 4% of the total British population. Table 5 summarises the numbers of each species of wader and wildfowl wintering in Suffolk over the last three years.

In addition to the BOEE data, obtained by counting high tide roost sites, the Deben, Stour and in particular, the Orwell, have been studied in even greater detail. The SWT and Landguard Bird Observatory have carried out detailed studies to assess the environmental impact on feeding waders and wildfowl of the loss of Fagbury mudflats and saltmarsh. Over the winters of 1984/85 and 1985/86 Fagbury provided feeding grounds for up to 80% of the oystercatcher, 41% of the dunlin, 40% of the ringed plover and 36% of the grey plover on the Orwell, despite the fact that Fagbury only accounts for 7% of the total area of intertidal mudflat. The importance of this mudflat was further highlighted during severe weather conditions when many waders and wildfowl from other feeding grounds, which may have frozen, move onto Fagbury which remains relatively frost free due to its position at the mouth of the estuary.

D. N. Bakewell

Shelduck.

A detailed understanding of the distribution and movements of waders and wildfowl utilising the mudflats of the Orwell (both from roost and feeding counts) has enabled us to assess the impact of any activity or development elsewhere on the estuary. Comparison of this data with the studies of the invertebrate fauna further our understanding of the ecology of the system and help identify any population fluctuations that occur. Such complementary studies are currently under way on the Deben and are planned for all the other Suffolk estuaries.

Botanical interest of Mudflats

Few plants can tolerate the conditions that prevail in estuaries, and only one group of true flowering plants, eel-grasses, have been able to colonise the intertidal mudflats below the lower limits of saltmarsh. The other major category of plants inhabiting mudflats are algae, including microscopic algae within the sediment, filamentous green algae (predominantly *Enteromorpha* and *Ulva sp.*) on the mud surface, and seaweeds (30 species have been recorded on the Suffolk estuaries) where rocky outcrops, seawalls or other artificial constructions provide a firm substrate for attachment. Both eel-grasses and filamentous algae play a particularly important role in trapping and binding sediment, facilitating accretion and preventing erosion. The mucus secreted by microscopic algae also aids the binding of sediment.

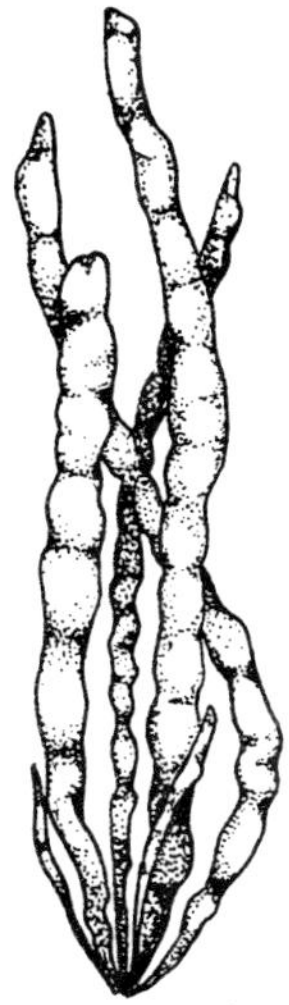

Enteromorpha

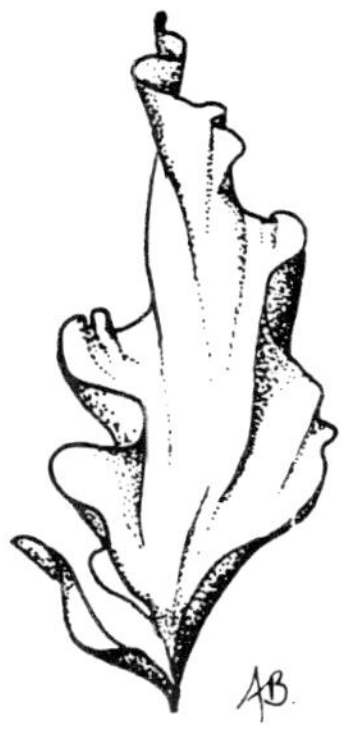

Ulva

A. W. Boyle

The presence of these plant communities therefore strongly influences the levels of accretion and erosion of mudflats. During 1931/2 many beds of eel-grass on both sides of the Atlantic suffered a severe wasting disease caused by a parasitic bacterium or fungus. As a direct result many estuaries experienced severe erosion of intertidal mudflats. In Suffolk it has been estimated that the Stour estuary lost some 15 million cubic metres of sediment between 1925 and 1965. Such severe erosion will have caused many changes in the physical and ecological characteristics of the estuary and is calculated to have resulted in a 30% increase in the tidal volume and the exposure of oyster beds thought to be 500 years old. Although it is important to monitor the intertidal mud surface plant communities, few studies have investigated this aspect of the Suffolk estuaries. Due to the importance of eel-grasses and *Enteromorpha* as a food source for wildfowl (particularly brent geese and wigeon) the Institute of Terrestial Ecology (ITE) studied, in some detail, the beds of these plant communities on the Stour and Orwell, as part of the Maplin Report, 1973.

All three species of eel-grass (common, narrow-leaved and dwarf) have been recorded in Suffolk. Common eel-grass is rarely found in estuaries and is now scarce in the county. The ITE study identified the flats between Nacton to Levington as the main eel-grass bed on the Orwell estuary. This was composed primarily of narrow-leaved eel-grass, but with a strip of dwarf eel-grass on the more elevated, better drained areas close to the shore. Narrow-leaved eel-grass was not found elsewhere on the estuary but dwarf eel-grass was located at three other sites, all on the south shore (figure 10). In 1973 eel-grass beds covered 99 hectares out of the total 720 hectares of mudflat on the Orwell. *Enteromorpha* covered 142 hectares of intertidal mudflat.

On the Stour eel-grass covered 244 hectares, of which narrow-leaved accounted for the majority (199 hectares, see figure 10). *Enteromorpha* was found to cover a total of 219 hectares.

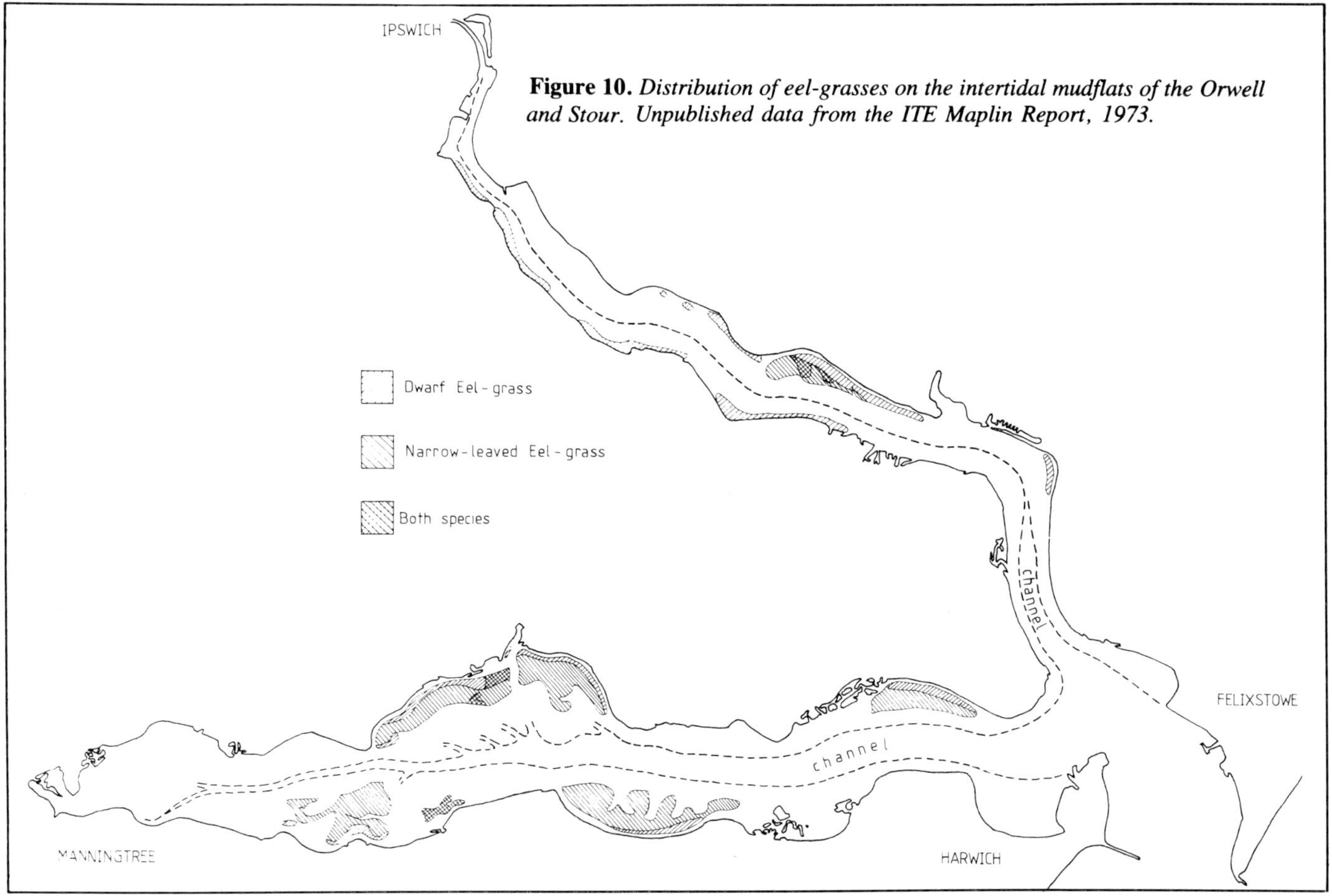

Figure 10. *Distribution of eel-grasses on the intertidal mudflats of the Orwell and Stour. Unpublished data from the ITE Maplin Report, 1973.*

It is important to note that narrow-leaved eel-grass dies back during the winter, whereas dwarf eel-grass is more or less evergreen and hence present during the winter for grazing wildfowl.

No studies have mapped the areas covered by eel-grasses or Enteromorpha in the other estuaries, although narrow-leaved eel-grass is known to occur in the Deben, Ore and Blyth. Dwarf eel-grass has only been recorded in the Orwell and Stour estuaries.

Saltmarsh

Ecology of Saltmarsh

Saltmarshes can be defined as areas of alluvial or peat deposits colonized by salt tolerant vegetation which is frequently inundated with saline water. They are one of the most natural habitats in Britain, and represent an important transitional community between true terrestrial vegetation and intertidal mudflats.

FORMATION OF SALTMARSH

Saltmarshes develop in sheltered parts of estuaries where wave energy is sufficiently dissipated to allow the accretion of sediment. When the level of the mudflat rises above the mean high water of neap tides (MHWN) a few species of plants are able to establish. This vegetation enhances further deposition of silt by trapping and binding the sediment and reducing wave scour of the surface layers. Mucus secreted by microscopic algae may also help stabilize the sediment. As the mud surface rises, a succession of plant species that are less able to tolerate tidal inundation colonise the marsh. Accretion may continue until the marsh surface is only reached by the highest tides.

The rate of saltmarsh formation is determined primarily by the degree of shelter, and the supply of suspended material. Rates of deposition can vary from a few millimetres to several centimetres per year. As in the case of mudflats there is a marked seasonality to accretion, most sedimentation taking place during the summer and autumn. Sedimentation is greatest on the low marsh, which is covered most frequently and for longer periods by the tide. Erosion of saltmarshes will occur when removal of sediment by the tide exceeds deposition (see chapter 3).

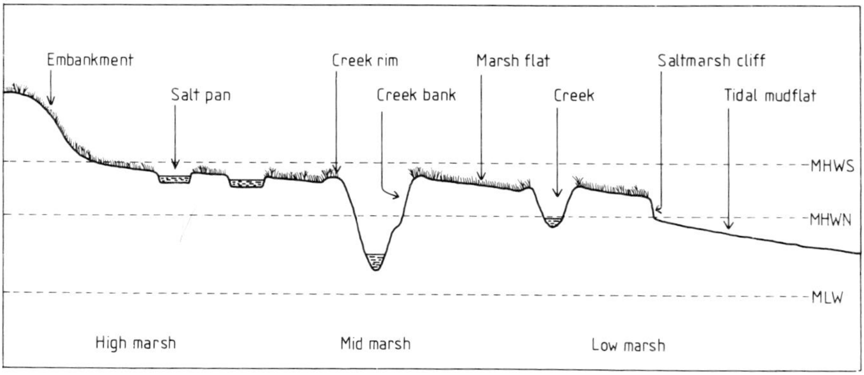

R. C. Dryden

Generalized profile of a saltmarsh.

Saltmarshes typically contain a number of sub-habitats of which the most extensive is the level marsh surface, or marsh flat. Tidal drainage creeks form a complex network of steep-sided channels which extend throughout the marsh. The base and sides of creeks are subject to high levels of scour from the ebb and flow of the tide and so tend to be bare of vegetation. Bare depressions in the marsh surface, known as salt pans, are another characteristic sub-habitat of the saltmarsh. Pans probably develop from depressions which existed in the marsh at the time of their initial colonization. Localized smothering of saltmarsh vegetation by tidal litter, followed by erosion of the resultant bare areas, can also lead to pan formation. Pans often contain standing water, the salinity of which can vary widely. After spring tides they may contain seawater, whilst after heavy rain the salinity may approach that of freshwater. During periods of high evaporation and low tides salinity can far exceed that of seawater and complete drying out can occur. High levels of salinity, combined with frequent waterlogging of the soil, probably account for the absence of rooted vegetation in pans.

SALTMARSH FLORA

The overriding factor influencing saltmarsh communities is the frequency and duration of tidal submergence. Saltmarshes are typically divided into three zones on the basis of altitude with respect to tidal height — the low, middle and high marsh. Each zone is characterized by a different assemblage of flowering plants and their associated communities. The low marsh or pioneer zone contains a sparse growth of a few species such as cord-grass, glasswort and sea aster. The middle marsh contains a greater diversity of species including sea purslane, sea lavender, sea arrow-grass and saltmarsh grass. These species are partially replaced on the high marsh by plants such as sea beet and sea couch which can only withstand infrequent submergence in sea water. Under natural circumstances the high marsh would grade into woodland, but this succession is normally prevented by the presence of a sea wall.

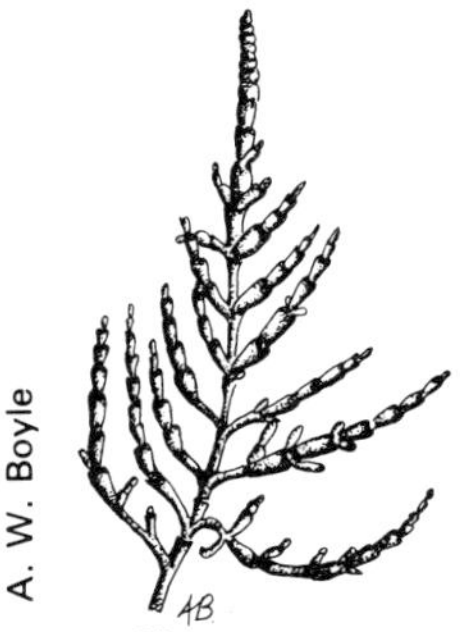

Glasswort.

Saltmarsh plants are highly specialised, and have adaptations enabling them to cope with three major sources of environmental stress, namely submergence by the tides, waterlogging and high salinity.

The leaves of many saltmarsh species, for example sea purslane and sea lavender, are thick and rubbery and so protected from mechanical damage caused by the flow of the tides. In addition many species possess a waxy leaf surface that is impermeable to water, preventing desiccation.

Soil waterlogging is characteristic of the lower marsh since this region is most frequently inundated by the tide. Waterlogging causes oxygen starvation and can lead to the death of plant root systems. Saltmarsh plants tolerate waterlogging by producing roots in the better drained surface layers of the soil, and/or by developing large air cavities in the deeper roots.

Some saltmarsh plants, such as thrift, sea lavender and cord-grasses, overcome

Sea lavender.

the problems associated with high salinity by actively excreting the excess salt that accumulates in their tissues during growth. Salt excretion is particularly efficient in cord-grasses, and may in part explain their ability to colonize the lowest levels of the marsh.

SALTMARSH FAUNA

Few animals have adapted to the harsh conditions that prevail within saltmarshes. Terrestrial animals have to cope with tidal inundation and high levels of salt. Some terrestrial invertebrates have activity rhythms which are in synchrony with the tides. Certain beetles, for example, retreat into burrows during periods of tidal inundation and so avoid being swept away. Saltmarsh spiders may have hairs which trap air bubbles and enable them to breath whilst submerged. Other terrestrial species, for example the larvae of saltmarsh moths, bypass the problems of submergence altogether by living within the tissue of the host plant.

Aquatic animals living on saltmarshes have to cope with salinity fluctuations and desiccation during exposure at low tide. Mud-dwelling invertebrates, requiring water to breath through their gills, may be exposed to the air for long periods while the tide is out, preventing breathing and causing desiccation. Desiccation can be avoided by burrowing deep into the sediment, whilst the effects of oxygen starvation can be minimized by the animal becoming quiescent, and so reducing its oxygen demands. The lugworm is capable of breathing in both air and under certain circumstances water.

Studies by the University of Essex on a cord-grass dominated saltmarsh at Seafield Bay, on the Stour, identified fifteen species of invertebrates in the sediment. The most abundant were ragworms, *Corophium volutator*, the worm *Tubifex costatus* and *Hydrobia ulvae*. Ragworms contributed between fifty-five and eighty-six percent of the total animal biomass and the common shore crab was found at densities of up to 169 per square metre.

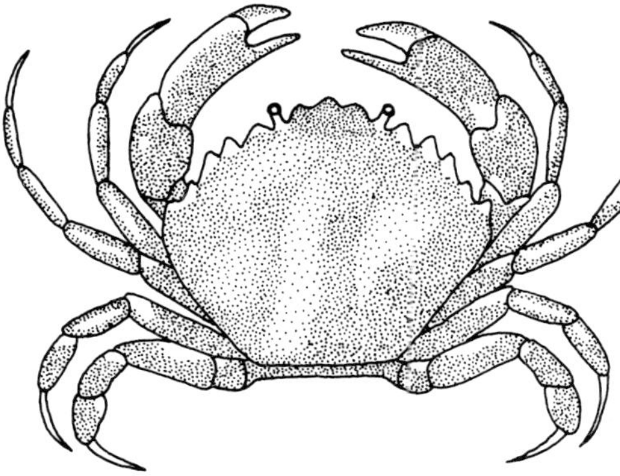

R. C. Dryden

Common shore crab.

Saltmarshes are highly productive ecosystems. Much of this productivity may be exported in the form of detritus to the adjacent mudflats and coastal waters, so enriching the invertebrate fauna and its predators.

Saltmarsh in Suffolk

In Britain there are approximately 40,000 hectares of saltmarsh, of which 816 hectares (just over 2%) occur in Suffolk. The distribution of saltmarsh between the Suffolk estuaries is shown in table 1. The largest area is on the Deben, which, despite its small size, has almost a third of the total saltmarsh. The Stour and Orwell only have small areas of saltmarsh in relation to their size. Of the 74 hectares on the Orwell, 14.5 hectares (almost 20%) is at Fagbury and will be destroyed during the building of the Felixstowe Dock extension.

Whilst vast areas of saltmarsh were reclaimed many years ago (see chapter 1 and table 2), some estuaries have also experienced a continued loss during the present century. For instance the area of saltmarsh on the Orwell today is only half of that shown on the tithe maps in the 1840's. In contrast the area of saltmarsh on the Deben has increased from 182 hectares in the 1840's to 251 hectares at the present day. This increase can be attributed to breaches in the sea wall at Hemley, Sutton and Bromeswell, rather than to accretion of new marsh over existing areas of mudflat. Indeed the areas of mature saltmarsh above the mean high water mark have stayed remarkably stable over the last 140 years.

Large areas of saltmarsh in Britain are now dominated by *Spartina anglica* (common cord-grass). This species was first discovered in Southampton Water in 1872 and is thought to have arisen from a hybrid between *Spartina maritima*, our native cord-grass, and *Spartina alterniflora*, an introduced species from North America. Unlike *Spartina maritima*, *Spartina anglica* is highly fertile, capable of vigorous growth, and can rapidly colonize large areas of previously bare intertidal mudflats. The rapid spread of *Spartina anglica*, which now covers some 12,000 hectares of marsh in Britain, is the result of deliberate planting (to promote reclamation and prevent erosion) as well as natural colonization. Some areas of *Spartina anglica* are experiencing "die-back", in which large areas of marsh degenerate, resulting in severe erosion. The exact causes of "die-back" are unknown, but are related to poor drainage conditions in the soil.

Spartina anglica colonizing bare mud at Manningtree on the Stour.

In Suffolk, *Spartina anglica* was planted in the Stour estuary at Brantham in 1923 and at Stutton in 1927-28. There is some evidence of planting in the Deben in 1929, and planting on the Alde occurred in 1934. Natural colonization of the Orwell occurred between 1940 and 1950. *Spartina anglica* has since spread rapidly in all these areas and now covers some 48% of the saltmarsh on the north shore of the Stour, 9% of the saltmarsh in the Orwell, 13% in the Deben and 10% in the Alde. Some "die-back" has been observed at Mistley and in other areas on the Stour. In contrast, our native cord-grass, *Spartina maritima*, is a rare plant of Suffolk saltmarshes, occurring sporadically on all of the estuaries with the exception of the Blyth. On the Orwell it is found at Trimley in both pioneer and established marsh, and on account of this the Maplin Report (see chapter 2) ranked this site one of the nine most important saltmarshes in south-east England.

The spread of *Spartina anglica* is of concern for two reasons. Firstly, it can result in the loss of large areas of intertidal mudflats, substantially reducing the feeding grounds available to waders and wildfowl. For example, in the Dyfi estuary in Wales, the rapid expansion of Spartina anglica over areas of bare mudflat during the 1970's was closely correlated with a steep decline in the numbers of certain waders, particularly oystercatcher and dunlin. Secondly, Spartina anglica can invade existing areas of saltmarsh at any level of the shore, out-competing native saltmarsh plants and excluding the normal communities that exist within the marsh.

In 1985 the NCC carried out a botanical survey of all saltmarsh in Suffolk with the exception of the Blyth and a small area on the Deben. This revealed that over three hundred hectares (24%) were low marsh colonised by pioneer species (cord-grass, glasswort and sea aster). A similar area was dominated by either sea lavender, sea purslane or thrift, species that inhabit middle marsh. Saltmarsh grass, which is capable of colonising both middle and high marsh, was found on 48% of the total area of saltmarsh. Areas of high marsh were found to be the scarcest saltmarsh communities in Suffolk, possibly because these are the first to be reclaimed. Rare saltmarsh plants which are found in Suffolk include Spartina maritima, lax-flowered sea lavender, rock sea lavender, golden samphire, and sea heath.

A. W. Boyle

Spartina maritima.

The saltmarshes of Suffolk are of considerable importance for birds. Saltmarsh plants provide grazing for overwintering flocks of wigeon and dark bellied brent geese, and the prolific supply of seed is exploited by large flocks of passerines, particularly linnet and twite. Areas of high marsh also provide secure roosting sites for waders, that are remote from human disturbance. The majority of important roost sites are found on areas of mature saltmarsh, for instance Waldringfield on the Deben, Fagbury on the Orwell and Deep Fleet on the Stour.

D. N. Bakewell

Twite.

Saltmarshes also provide valuable sites for breeding waders. The main species nesting in Suffolk are redshank, oystercatcher, avocet, black-headed gull, skylark, meadow pipit, and more recently Canada geese. In 1985 a breeding redshank survey conducted by the RSPB and the NCC recorded an exceptionally high density of nests in a plot of saltmarsh on the Deben. The overall importance of the Suffolk estuaries for breeding waders is, however, unknown and as a result the SWT Estuaries Project has coordinated a detailed survey of breeding waders on all saltmarsh in Suffolk (spring/summer 1988).

Shingle

Ecology of Shingle

Shingle is classified as sediment in which the particle size is intermediate between that of small boulders and sand. Approximately 900 kilometres of the British coastline is bordered by pure shingle much of which is too mobile for vegetation to establish. Nevertheless, Britain is particularly important for vegetated shingle, possessing one third of the total area in Europe. In Suffolk there are two major shingle features associated with the estuaries. These are Orfordness, the second largest area of vegetated shingle in Britain and the finest example in Europe of a vegetated shingle spit, and Landguard. All of Suffolk's estuaries contain shingle within the sediment at their mouth, and it is shingle barriers that have enclosed the former estuaries of the Minsmere, Dunwich, Benacre and Hundred rivers.

The intertidal zone on shingle structures is too mobile for vegetation to establish. Above the high tide mark where the shingle is relatively stable certain species are able to survive. These plants encounter many problems, especially in connection with water availability, the lack of nutrients, and exposure to coastal winds and salt spray. Shingle flora therefore contains many specialist species that tend to be rare or very localised in distribution. The plant communities colonizing an area of shingle are influenced by the length of time the shingle has remained undisturbed and the amount of fine particles (organic and inorganic) that have accumulated between the pebbles.

D. L. Cheyne

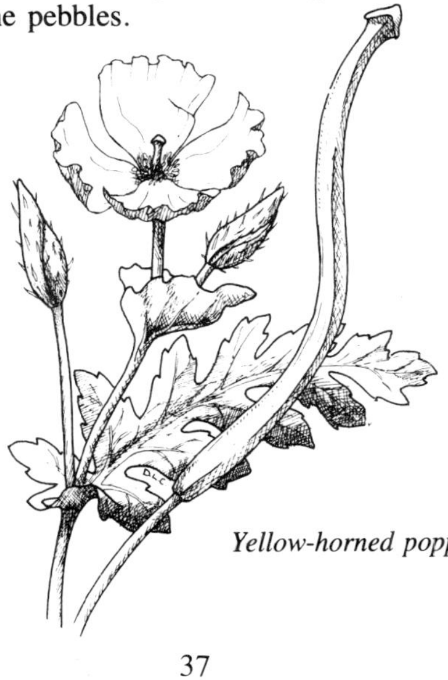

Yellow-horned poppy.

Vegetation occurs predominantly on areas of fine shingle and tends not to occur in coarse pebbles where seeds may fall too deep to germinate. If germination is successful in coarse shingle, seedlings are often unable to tolerate periods of drought. Once pioneer species have established (for example, sea pea, sea kale, yellow-horned poppy) and the shingle stabilised, humus is produced from the build-up of decaying roots and shoots, as well as through the trapping of debris, facilitating the establishment of a succession of species less well adapted to shingle. Drift material also promotes the establishment of vegetation, enriching the shingle sufficiently for pioneer species to establish. On the more established and stable areas a thin turf of acid shingle heath may develop, supporting a wide variety of species including rareties as well as plants that are commonly found on acid grassland elsewhere. Shingle heath often contains areas dominated by lichens and mosses.

Botanical Interest of Estuarine Shingle in Suffolk

Both Orfordness and Landguard have been designated as SSSI's for their rare and nationally important plant communities. Orfordness is also a National Nature Reserve managed by the NCC and Landguard a Local Nature Reserve managed by the SWT. Botanical surveys of Landguard have identified 375 species of flowering plant, and it is the only site in Britain for stinking goosefoot.

Sea pea is a particularly important component of the Suffolk shingle flora, occurring on our coast in greater quantity than anywhere else in Western Europe. Orfordness is one of the few areas in Britain where this species is recognised to be increasing. Other plant species of note include sea kale, yellow-horned poppy, sea spurge, yellow vetch, sea campion, sea holly and a number of rare clovers.

D. L. Cheyne

Sea pea.

Fauna of Suffolk Shingle

The shingle areas associated with the Suffolk estuaries are of particular importance for breeding birds. Both Orfordness and Landguard hold large breeding colonies of little tern. Orfordness also provides the habitat for breeding oyster-catchers, ringed plovers, avocets and a colony of approximately 8,000 pairs of lesser-black backed gulls and 2,000 pairs of herring gulls. Such large populations of breeding birds cause substantial nutrient enrichment of the shingle, promoting the establishment of permanent plant cover.

Other species of note include three rare spiders recorded on Orfordness and the fauna inhabiting the brackish lagoons at Shingle Street. The latter includes the sea anenome, *Nematostella vectensis*, found in only two other sites in Britain.

Little terns.

D. N. Bakewell

Grazing Marshes

Coastal grazing marshes and their associated dyke systems are an important habitat for many estuarine species. They lie at or below sea level, and are almost all enclosed by seawalls, having originally been reclaimed from saltmarsh. Grazing marshes, particularly those which are unimproved, are especially important for breeding, roosting and feeding waders.

During spring and summer the grazing marshes of Suffolk provide nest sites for large numbers of waders and wildfowl and in particular redshank and lapwing. The high water table characteristic of unimproved marshes softens the ground, encouraging earthworms and other invertebrates into the upper levels of the soil where they are accessible to feeding birds. During the winter large flocks of waders and wildfowl may use the grazing marshes for feeding, especially at high water when the adjacent mudflats are covered by the tide. Grazing marshes are also

important as roosting sites, particularly during spring tides when traditional saltmarsh sites are submerged.

From the time of their enclosure until 1953 there was little alteration in either the use or management of coastal marshes. Mostly they provided poor grazing, and very little arable cultivation was attempted. Soil conditions were wet due to the low-lying nature of the land, and large areas were frequently inundated by seawater which either overtopped the seawalls or entered through breaches. The disastrous sea floods of January 1953 resulted in the submergence of 8097 hectares of coastal marshes in Suffolk, and much of this land lay idle for years afterwards.

The floods provided the impetus to begin large-scale agricultural improvements to the grazing marshes. The seawalls were strengthened and raised in height, and pumps were installed to lower the water level in the dykes. Lowering of the water table enabled underdrainage of the marshes, and fields were levelled to remove gullies (often the remnants of saltmarsh creeks), thereby allowing the efficient operation of farm machinery. The combined effects of levelling and drainage made it possible to convert many grazing marshes to arable farmland. Between 1955 and 1958, 20% of the grazing marshes in Suffolk were coverted to arable, and significant losses have occurred since. Much of the grazing marsh that remains today has improved drainage and as a consequence is of little value to wildlife.

The marshes adjoining the estuaries of the Blyth and the Alde/Ore/Butley complex have been designated by the Ministry of Agriculture, Fisheries and Food as part of the Suffolk River Valleys Environmentally Sensitive Area (see figure 7). Farmers can voluntarily enter into an agreement in which they receive payment for adopting or maintaining traditional farming practices on areas of grassland. Additional management guidelines designed to benefit wildlife attract a higher level of payment. Such guidelines include the maintenance of a high water table, restrictions on grazing and the use of machinery during the breeding season, and controls on the use of pesticides and inorganic fertilisers. Payments are also offered for converting arable land to grassland. It is hoped that the introduction of the Suffolk River Valleys ESA will increase the value of these areas for breeding waders.

Chapter 3 The Impact of Human Activities on the Suffolk Estuaries

Introduction

All human activities on estuaries cause some modification or disturbance, the impact of which may be small or highly significant. The major reclamation projects of the past have dramatically altered our estuaries and destroyed large areas of the intertidal zone. Other activities such as local fishing and shellfish harvesting are largely sustainable and so have had little environmental impact.

Today estuaries are under pressure from many directions. Tidal power barrages, marinas, roads and bridges, dock developments, and amenity lakes are amongst the most prominent developments threatening some thirty of the major estuaries around Britain. Additional pressures arise from increased commercial and recreational activities, tipping of refuse, dumping of dredge spoil and the discharge of excessive quantities of industrial and domestic effluents.

Although the impact of many small developments and activities may on the surface appear insignificant, they collectively result in the steady deterioration of the estuarine environment.

Not all the above problems relate to the Suffolk estuaries. Many, however, are relevant and are discussed below.

Pollution

Pollution can be defined as the human introduction of any substance or energy (for example heat) into the environment that causes harmful effects to living organisms.

Throughout history estuaries have been used for the disposal of a variety of waste products originating both from industrial processes and domestic sources. Other pollutants enter either by accident (e.g. oil spills) or from the river catchment (e.g. fertilisers and pesticides). There are, however, many inherent problems in releasing potentially harmful substances into estuaries. The influence of the tides extends the time a pollutant may remain in the estuary. For instance in the Thames at London Bridge the downstream flow as the tide retreats is 15 kilometres, compared with an upstream flow with the flood of 13 kilometres, giving a net seaward movement of only 2 kilometres per tidal cycle. Estimates for the flushing times of the Suffolk estuaries vary from 20 hours to 44 days according to the season and the source of information. Despite these discrepancies, the residence time for effluents released into the estuaries may be days or even weeks, during which time many substances may become fixed within the sediment or concentrated by mud-dwelling organisms.

Anglian Water regularly analyse both water and sediment samples from all the Suffolk estuaries to assess their water quality and pollution status. Of all the estuaries in the Anglian Water region, stretching from the Humber to south Essex, only the upper reaches of the Orwell estuary are graded as class 4, the most polluted. The remainder of the Suffolk estuaries are class 3 (lower reaches of the Orwell), class 2 (upper reaches of the Deben), and class 1 (Blyth, Alde/Ore/Butley, Stour and the Deben).

The following section reviews pollution on the Suffolk estuaries.

Organic effluent

Traditionally estuaries have been used for the dilution and dispersal of domestic sewage derived from the adjacent towns and villages. The Suffolk estuaries are no exception, with 10 outfalls into the Stour, 23 into the Orwell, 7 into the Deben, 4 into the Alde/Ore/Butley and 2 into the Blyth (figure 11). Most sewage effluent is discharged untreated or with primary treatment only (settlement and removal of larger material). The discharge of sewage into estuaries can increase productivity within the ecosystem provided only small quantities are released and there is enough oxygen to facilitate decomposition. There is however a threshold beyond which further enrichment may cause pollution. The decomposition of excessive quantities of organic material by bacteria depletes oxygen from the water and sediment, causing the extinction of the normal invertebrate fauna. This phenomenon may be exaggerated during the summer when the river flow is at its lowest, the water temperature is highest and the flushing time is long. The discharge of

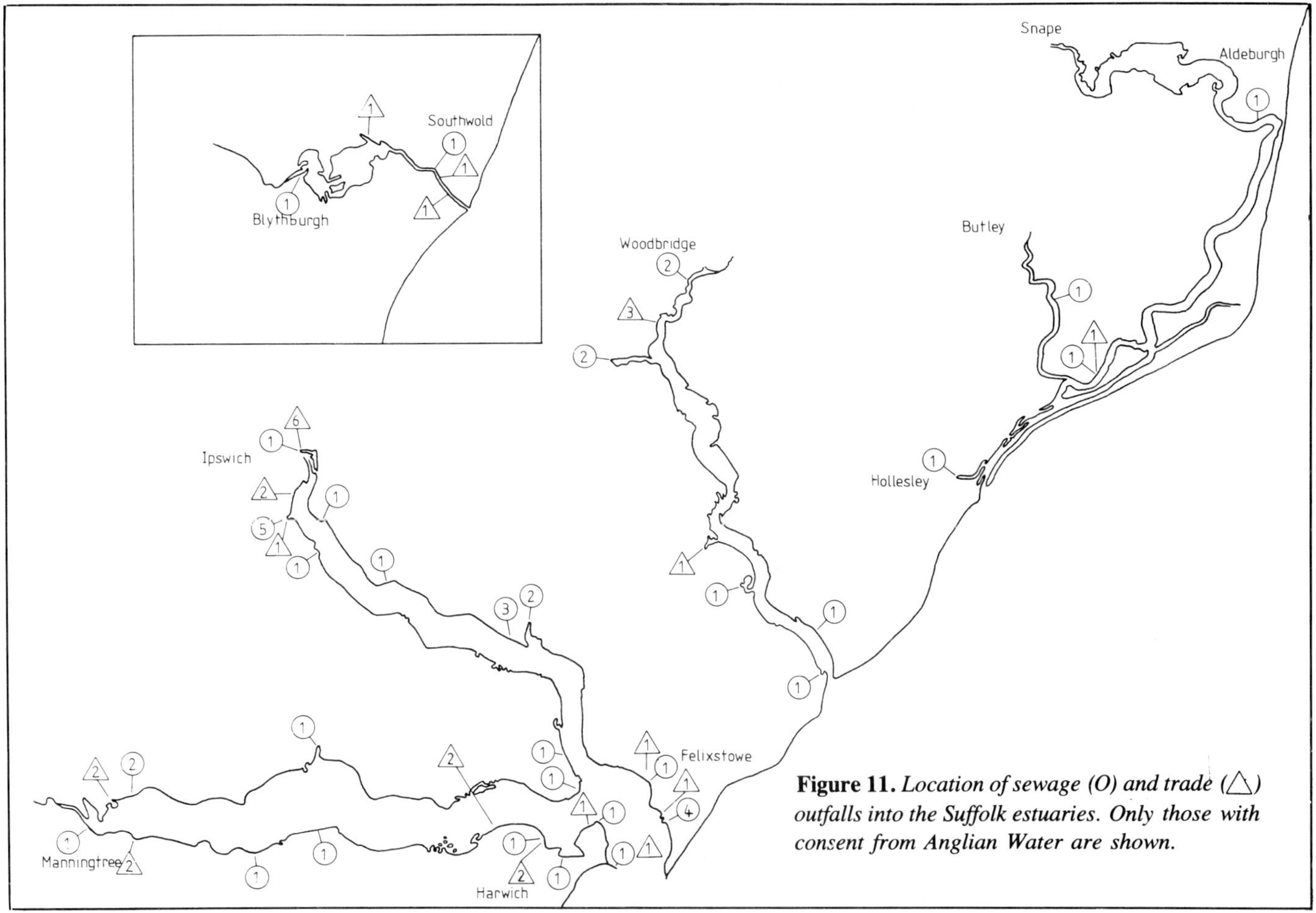

Figure 11. *Location of sewage (O) and trade (△) outfalls into the Suffolk estuaries. Only those with consent from Anglian Water are shown.*

large volumes of effluent from a single point can cause severe oxygen depletion in a localised area.

During the summer when rainfall is low and the extraction of river water for irrigation is high, the amount of freshwater reaching the Orwell estuary from the River Gipping can be less than half the volume of sewage discharged from the single outfall at Cliff Quay, in the upper reaches of the Orwell. This relatively large discharge, coupled with organic effluent from industrial sources and the long flushing time of the Orwell (conflicting estimates suggest that this may be between 3.5 and 44 days), creates completely anoxic conditions in the sediment of the upper estuary.

Cliff Quay sewage outfall. Solids are removed by boat and dumped at sea.

The influence of organic pollution on mud-dwelling invertebrates differs between species. Some are only found in clean water, whereas others can tolerate slight pollution (for instance *Corophium volutator*, some species of shrimp, *Hydrobia ulvae*, and cockles). Some species become more dominant as the pollution level rises, but are unable to tolerate high levels of enrichment (for instance ragworm, baltic tellin). Only a few species, such as some oligochaete worms, can tolerate the highest levels of pollution and indeed their presence indicates poor water quality.

It is interesting to note that over the last fifteen years the populations of cockle and *Hydrobia ulvae* in the Orwell estuary have decreased, whilst the ragworm has become more abundant. These changes are concomitant with an estimated 15% increase in the output of Cliff Quay sewage outfall (see chapter 2).

Excessive nutrient enrichment also promotes the growth of green algae (particularly *Enteromorpha* and *Ulva*), which forms a blanket cover of intertidal mudflats and saltmarsh. Such growths smother the invertebrate fauna of mudflats, and may inhibit, or in some cases kill, saltmarsh vegetation.

Heavy metals and pesticides

Many effluents released into estuaries for dilution and dispersal contain heavy metals (e.g. mercury, arsenic, lead, selenium and tin) that may be reconcentrated either by sedimentary or biological processes. Biological concentration first occurs in animals that filter food particles from water, but is further magnified in animals higher in the food chain (invertebrate predators, birds and fish). Heavy metals, however, are also adsorbed on to suspended particles of silt which can settle and remain in the sediment for protracted periods.

Some metals are a natural constituent of sea water and many are essential for normal life processes. Heavy metals are generally not required for metabolic activity and are toxic at quite low concentrations. Other metals (e.g. iron, copper, cobalt, and manganese), which are necessary for normal metabolic processes, become toxic at high concentrations. The largest input of heavy metals into our estuaries is from sewage and industrial effluent and may cause a number of sub-lethal effects on estuarine organisms. Data on the toxicity of many heavy metals is however sadly limited, but some are known to cause sub-lethal effects in the embryonic stages of fish (arsenic), molluscs and shrimps (lead, zinc), inhibit algal growth and enzyme activities in jellyfish (cadmium), and decrease the diversity of microscopic algae (nickel).

The level of metals in the sediment and water of the Suffolk estuaries is within the quality standards accepted by Anglian Water. However, sedimentary levels of mercury in the upper reaches of the Orwell are still high as a result of a historic industrial source no longer discharging into the estuary. The effects of this are unknown.

Pesticides are toxic by design and whilst these chemicals are diluted many times upon reaching our estuaries, they are persistent and accumulate within the sediment, plants and animals. The concentration of pesticides in estuaries can be five to ten times greater than offshore. Nothing is known about the levels of pesticides in the Suffolk estuaries.

Anti-fouling paints

Anti-fouling paints are designed to kill marine organisms that bind to boat hulls. By 1986 it was evident that marine life was being severely affected where a high density of boats were moored in shallow or semi-enclosed water. The effects of tri-butyl tin (TBT-oxide is the active ingredient in most anti-fouling paints since the early 1970's) on selected marine organisms are now well documented and known to occur at extremely low concentrations. Such concentrations are also known to exist in many marinas and estuaries in Britain, and especially where there is a high density of moored boats.

TBT may enter the water from many sources (leaching directly from paints, paint scrapings, accidental spillage whilst painting, or boat washing) and has a strong tendency to become adsorbed onto particulate matter, therefore becoming fixed within the sediment. Abnormalities attributed to TBT poisoning have been found in the pacific oyster and other molluscs, where shell thickening, a decrease in body weight and reproductive failure are experienced. TBT has also been found to affect the mudsnail *Nassarius obsoletus*, limpets, periwinkles and dogwhelks.

Over three thousand leisure craft are moored on the Orwell.

In the latter, TBT causes a phenomenon known as imposex where the female whelk takes on male characteristics, which disrupt reproductive success. In Plymouth Sound a dramatic increase in the incidence of imposex in dogwhelks coincided with the increased usage of TBT anti-fouling paints. The recent decline in our native oyster, now at an all time low, is at least partly attributed to TBT.

In January 1987 the Government banned the "retail sale and the supply for retail sale" of organotin anti-fouling paints and set a target water quality standard of 0.02 micrograms TBT per litre of water. However, even these concentrations are known to reduce the growth rate of our native oyster, and concentrations as low as 0.003 micrograms per litre of water are reported to cause imposex in dogwhelks. It is hoped that the Government will introduce a legally binding Environmental Quality Standard ten times lower than the target level currently used.

The use of TBT paints has not been banned on boats larger than 25 metres and the input of TBT from ships has, in the past, received little attention. Studies in the USA suggest that moored ships can elevate levels of TBT in the adjacent water. In Britain MAFF is currently researching the levels of TBT released from ships at anchorage, in commercial harbours and in dry docks. The removal of old paint and repainting of large vessels in dry docks provides a potential source for localised pollution, although the majority of boats using the ports of Suffolk go elsewhere for repainting. The levels of TBT in water around ships at Felixstowe dock have been found to vary from 0.166 to less than 0.001 micrograms per litre depending on the ship.

The Port of Ipswich.

Ipswich port is the fourth largest container port in the UK and the sixth biggest roll-on/roll-off terminal, handling a total of 4.5 million tonnes in 2067 vessels (1986 figures). No studies have looked at TBT in either sediment or water around the dock. In the Stour, however, sediment samples have been analysed by AW who have found TBT concentrations that vary from undetectable levels to 283 micrograms per kilogram of sediment at Mistley. Elsewhere in Britain the levels of TBT in sediment can be 1000 to 10,000 times higher than in the water column, but it is unclear what impact this is having on mud-dwelling invertebrates.

With regard to Suffolk it is impossible to link, with any degree of certainty, the reported changes in the invertebrate fauna of the Stour and Orwell (chapter 2) with the introduction and use of TBT, although this has occurred over the same period.

Oil and petroleum products

Oil may be released into an estuary either by accident or as a continuous legal discharge authorised by Anglian Water (for instance there is one into the Gipping and one into the Stour). Oil and petroleum products may enter the Suffolk estuaries by spillage during unloading and loading, discharge of oil-contaminated bilge water (now illegal), collision of oil-carrying boats, discharges from shore-based storage installations and refineries, and run-off from roads and garage.

Oil pollution creates a number of problems within an estuary. The heavier fractions of oil are relatively inert but may still cause severe physical damage by smothering areas of mudflat and saltmarsh, killing both mud-dwelling invertebrates and vegetation. Saltmarsh acts as an oil trap and the plants within this community vary in their susceptibility to damage by oil. In general, annual species with shallow roots and minimal food reserves rarely recover (e.g. glasswort, annual seablite) whilst perennials, especially those with large tap roots (e.g. sea arrow-grass, sea plantain and thrift) are relatively tolerant. Filamentous green algae are quickly killed by oil pollution, but have the capacity to recover rapidly unless subjected to successive oil spills. Emulsifiers are often used to disperse oil spills, however, the chemical itself or the emulsifier/oil mixtures are often more toxic than the oil alone.

Many water soluble components of oil and petroleum products (especially diesel) are toxic to a broad spectrum of marine organisms and in particular the eggs, larvae and juvenile forms. These result in developmental abnormalities, as well as behavioural and metabolic changes. Long term effects are experienced when light oils penetrate into the sediment, a process that is enhanced by the presence of dispersants/emulsifiers.

On the Orwell, Powell Duffryn (a bulk storage company) operates 89,000 cubic metres of tankage for oil and chemical products at Ipswich Dock, handling over 300 ships a year. The company's throughput is approximately 650,000 tonnes of refined petroleum products a year, discharging from and to boats through a pipeline on Cliff Quay. Not surprisingly, concern has been expressed by the Harwich Harbour Board Pilotage Director (East Anglian Daily Times 12/5/88) over the possibility of tankers laden with "low flashpoint fuel . . . getting into trouble" as they navigate, sometimes without a pilot, through moored leisure craft on the 16 kilometres of the Orwell estuary. The effects of a spill, particularly of light diesel oils, within the confines of the estuary would be catastrophic.

The continuous discharge of oil into the estuary is more insidious. Over the last year a number of reports of light diesel oil spills have occurred. In November 1987, for example, spills resulted in a number of oiled swans (two of which died) and dead gulls in the dock region. Coinciding with this spill were reports of dead lugworms surfacing on the Black Ooze mudflats adjacent to Cliff Quay. A film of light oil is often evident on the water surface in the upper reaches of the estuary, and occasionally heavy oil is spilt in the wet dock.

Dock Activities and Channel Dredging

The estuaries of Suffolk provide navigable water for the ports of Harwich, Felixstowe and Ipswich. Activities associated with these docks have had a major impact on both the Stour and the Orwell.

Through the ages Ipswich has been one of the most prosperous ports in the country. The first records of a port date back to Roman times, but it was not until the 12th century that the wool trade expanded activities dramatically. The Orwell estuary has faced many periods of siltation (reported in the 10th, 16th, 17th and 19th centuries) that have threatened closure of the port, and the first records of "improvements" to the channel date back to 1614. Large-scale dredging did not take place until the early 1800's when the River Commission was set up to cure the problems associated with siltation. This resulted in "deepening, widening, cleansing and otherwise improving the river". By 1842 many of the mudflats above Cliff Reach and the Southern Marsh had been reclaimed, the enclosed dock built and the New Cut dredged, rechannelling the river alongside the new dock. In 1887 the dock acquired its first dredger and extensive work began straightening channels and increasing the navigable depths (see figure 12).

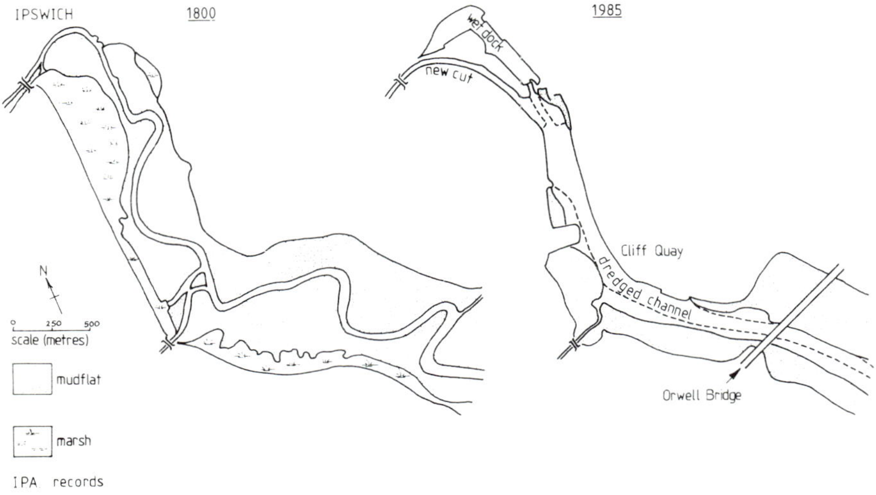

Figure 12. *The upper reaches of the Orwell estuary prior to dredging in 1800 and in 1985.*

Since 1947 three major dredging schemes have removed an estimated four million cubic metres of silt from the estuary, and maintenance dredging around the dock berths removes another 38,000 cubic metres each year. The channel is now cut to a depth of 5.8 metres, in some places extending down to the chalk bed, and stretches from Ipswich dock to Trimley, increasing the volume of the estuary by 56% (see figure 13). Today the river is dredged from Ipswich to Potters Reach every 5-10 years to remove sediment that has settled or slipped into the channel. Originally the dredged spoil was dumped in Gills Hole opposite Levington Creek, but now it is removed to sea and deposited six miles east of Felixstowe in an official dump licenced by MAFF.

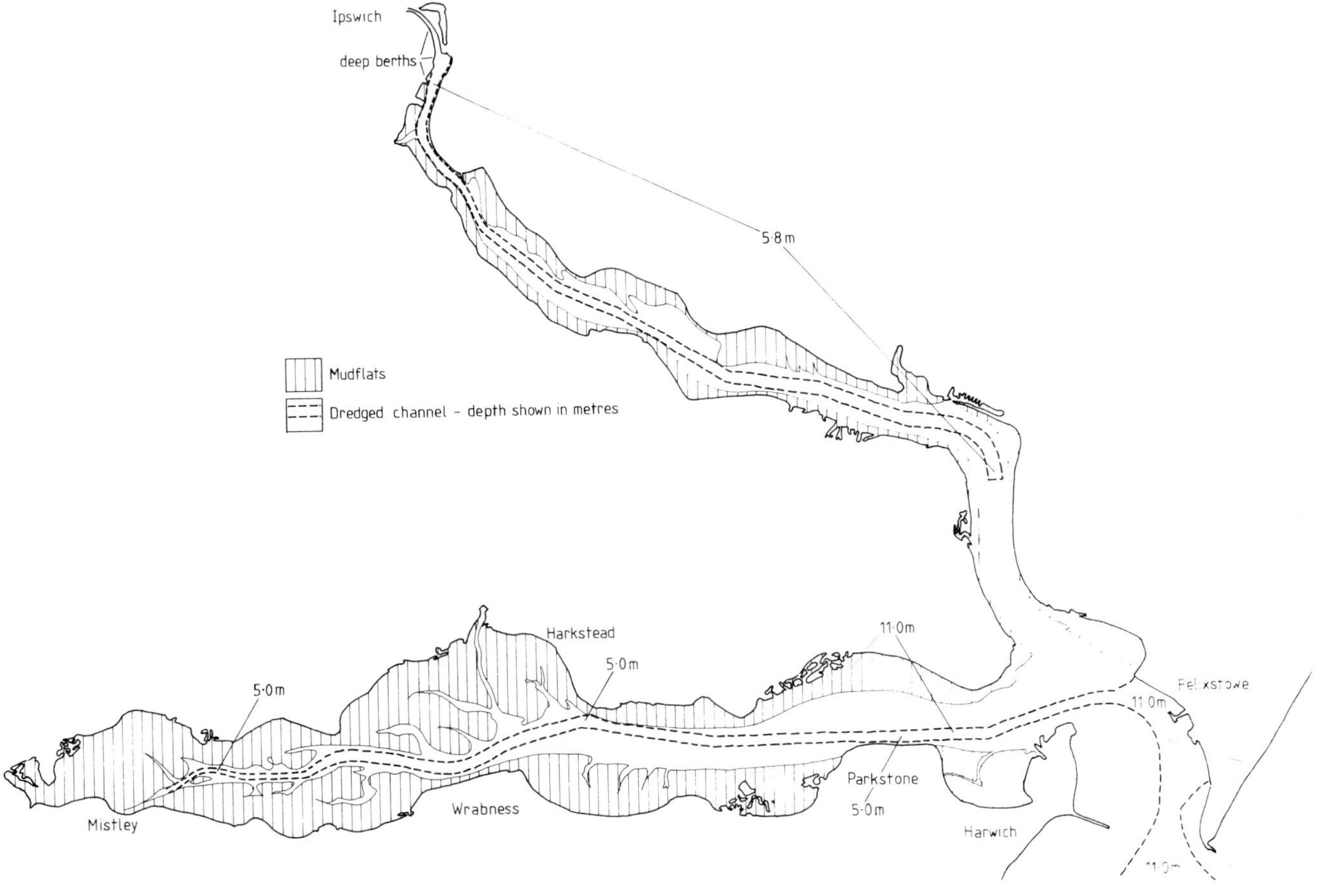

Figure 13. *The position of dredged channels on the Orwell and Stour.*

Dredging in the upper reaches of the Orwell, areas that would naturally be shallow and prone to sedimentation, has resulted in many changes in the physical characteristics of the estuary. Widening and straightening channels, coupled with a dramatic increase in shipping, has caused an increase in the energy of water penetrating the estuary, a net upstream movement of sediment towards the dock and the erosion of mudflats. At the dock the deep berths create a sediment trap, and consequently require continual dredging. Of the dredged material 39% is thought to originate from mudflat erosion. The quantity of sediment dredged and removed is estimated to be large in comparison with that imported with the tides and river. In summary, there is a net loss of sediment from the whole estuary, perpetuated by a cycle of mudflat erosion, siltation and dredging.

Gullies formed during mudflat erosion on the Orwell.

The Stour also has a history of dredging activities dating back to the 1850's. Between 1967 and 1975 five million cubic metres of sand and gravel were dredged from the central channel between Parkeston Quay and Harkstead, and by 1991 a further 1,500,000 cubic metres will have been extracted to cut a 5 metre deep channel between Wrabness and Mistley. The death of eel-grass (growing on the mudflats) is estimated to have caused the erosion and loss of another 15 million cubic metres of silt, between 1925 and 1965, resulting in a 30% increase in tidal volume. Channel dredging between Parkeston Quay and Mistley is thought to have accentuated slumping and scour of the intertidal mudflats (see figure 13).

Dredging boat on the Stour.

The physical characteristics of the estuaries have also been altered by extensive dredging at the mouth of the Stour and Orwell. The approaches to Harwich and Felixstowe, which were once prone to shoaling, are now capable of accommodating the world's largest container vessels. In 1984/5 the six mile entrance to the harbour was deepened from 8.9 metres to 11 metres, removing some 8.5 million cubic metres of sediment, and every year maintenance dredging continues to remove one million cubic metres of sediment from Harwich Harbour (including Felixstowe and Harwich Ports). Such changes will almost certainly increase the wave and tidal energy penetrating up the Orwell and Stour, altering the currents and patterns of sedimentation within the estuaries. Severe erosion of Shotley, Trimley, and Erwarton saltmarshes is already evident and may be the result of increased tidal scour causing the erosion of the adjacent mudflats. Severe erosion of Shotley mudflats during the last fifteen years may also help explain the decline and paucity of invertebrates in this area (chapter 2).

The disturbance of sediment during dredging causes an increase in the turbidity of the water, and the release of heavy metals and organic compounds that have accumulated within the mudflats. The resuspension of contaminated sediment results in a build up of heavy metals in invertebrates inhabiting the adjacent areas.

Reclamation

Reclamation of the Suffolk estuaries for agricultural land has been covered elsewhere in this report and is summarised in table 2. The total area of land reclaimed is estimated to be 10,817 hectares, and today only 875 hectares of saltmarsh and 3478 hectares of mudflat remain. Since the original reclamation schemes some areas have reverted to mudflat and saltmarsh due to breaches in the sea walls. For instance the Blyth estuary now contains approximately 250 hectares of intertidal mudflat that in 1840 were grazing marsh (figure 4). The floods of 1953 breached many seawalls around the Suffolk coast and caused the flooding of an estimated 8097 hectares of coastal grazing marsh. Some of these walls have never been repaired.

Breached seawall on the Blyth.

Today breaches in the sea walls exist on the Deben, Alde and Blyth estuaries. Further breaches are likely in the future, since many walls requiring maintenance work are being neglected. Indeed where neither people nor property are in danger funds are no longer available for the repair of sea defences due to recent cut-backs in funding. The consequences of breaches in the sea walls are of course devastating for the farmers involved, and where important grazing marshes are concerned, for instance Shotley marshes on the Orwell and Hazelwood marshes on the Alde, will also be detrimental to many aspects of estuarine wildlife. In other areas the return of land to the intertidal zone would be of direct benefit.

Over the last few decades reclamation on the Suffolk estuaries has largely been the result of dock developments. The most imminent development is the loss of a further 68 hectares of mudflat and 14.5 hectares of saltmarsh by the extension of Felixstowe Dock on the Orwell. At the other end of the estuary the West Bank

Terminal at Ipswich is being extended over another 15 hectares of mudflat. On the opposite bank the site of Ipswich Power Station is soon to be redeveloped for container handling and whilst this will not reclaim any more of the intertidal zone these two developments will almost certainly increase the number of ships using the estuary. Reclamation is also imminent on the Stour where approximately 100 hectares of mudflat at Bathside Bay is likely to be developed to extend Harwich harbour.

The impact of the direct loss of intertidal mudflat and saltmarsh is perhaps obvious, but the construction of harbours, quays and even piers, may cause more subtle changes in estuaries. For instance a quay projecting into the low water channel may cause substantial changes in water currents, influencing the patterns of sedimentation and salinity within the estuary and subsequently altering the distribution of fauna within the sediment. The effects of dredging alongside the quay, to accomodate large ships, has been covered elsewhere in this chapter.

Small-scale reclamation is also evident on the Suffolk estuaries and whilst the extension of yachting clubs, marinas and boat hards may seem insignificant in isolation, their accumulative effect over decades will be substantial.

Recreation

Since the early 1950s there has been a dramatic increase in organised water and land-based recreational pursuits associated with the estuaries. These include yachting, small dinghy sailing, water-skiing, wind-surfing, angling, canoeing, swimming, birdwatching, water scooting, wildfowling and walking. Their common impact on estuarine wildlife is one of disturbance, although individual pursuits may have additional effects.

Fortunately most activities occur in the summer when the numbers of waders and wildfowl on the estuaries are relatively small. Summer disturbance may, however, influence breeding birds especially where land and water-based activities approach sensitive areas of saltmarsh. The major impact on breeding waders and wildfowl comes from land-based leisure pursuits, for example dog walking and even insensitive birdwatching. Little terns nesting on accessible areas of shingle, for example Landguard and Orfordness, are particularly sensitive to disturbance. If the weather conditions are good on Whitsun bank holiday, when the little terns are incubating, the large number of walkers may cause the destruction or desertion of many nests. Tern colonies also suffer badly from egg collecting, and in some areas from destruction by scrambling bikes and four-wheel drive vehicles.

Yachting activities dominate many of the Suffolk estuaries in the summer, and the number of clubs and marinas has increased dramatically over the last few decades. All the estuaries, with the exception of the Blyth, provide swing moorings in the channels and on the mudflats as well as marina moorings. On the Orwell, for instance, there are a total of 3000 moored leisure craft, and the recent completion of the Shotley Marina will add a further 350. The development of a 1000 berth marina at Dovercourt on the coast south of Harwich will also increase the number of yachts using the Orwell and Stour as well as other east coast estuaries.

As a response to the increasing demand for marinas, a firm of consultants have recently been commissioned by English Estates to undertake a feasibility study to identify suitable sites for marina developments along the East Anglian coast. Other sources have already suggested areas on the Alde and Deben which could be developed as marinas.

The building of marinas within estuaries invariably involves the loss of mudflat and/or saltmarsh, but in addition to the direct loss of habitat, the adjacent areas of mudflat may also be deserted by some species of wader and wildfowl unable to tolerate disturbance.

Water-skiing is restricted to specific sites on the Orwell, Deben and Ore. The Wash from power boats may well increase the erosion of saltmarsh and noise may cause disturbance to wildlife.

Land-based leisure activities, such as walking, can often cause the destruction of vegetation by trampling. On saltmarshes this may lead to erosion and ultimately the complete loss of habitat. Shingle vegetation is particularly sensitive to trampling. On Chesil Beach in Dorset, for instance, the NCC have found that even low levels of visitor pressure inhibit colonisation of shingle by vegetation.

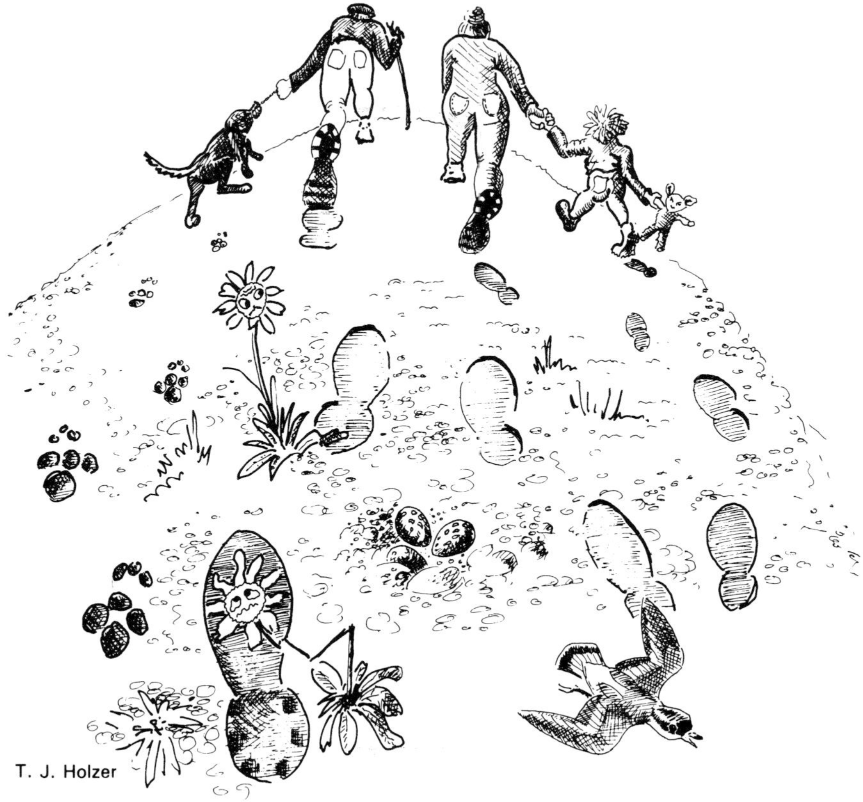

T. J. Holzer

C. H. Beardall

Plate 9. *Southwold Town Marshes.*

T. J. Holzer

Roger Tidman

Plate 10. *Grazing marshes provide valuable breeding sites for redshank.*

Roger Tidman

Plate 11. *Oystercatcher on nest.*

A. W. Boyle

Roger Tidman

Plate 12. *The Alde/Ore/Butley is internationally important for avocet.*

C. H. Beardell

Plate 13. *Fagbury mudflats. This area is soon to be destroyed by the building of the Felixstowe Dock extension.*

C. H. Beardall

Plate 14. *The upper reaches of the Orwell, the most polluted estuary in the Anglian Water region.*

C. H. Beardall

Plate 15. *Saltmarsh erosion at Trimley.*

C. H. Beardall

Plate 16. *The newly constructed marina at Shotley on the River Orwell.*

Bait-digging

The increase in popularity of sea angling in recent years has led to a corresponding increase in the demand for bait. This demand is largely satisfied by the collection of lugworms and ragworms from the intertidal sand and mudflats of estuaries. Apart from producing unsightly pits and trenches on the shore, bait-digging can have a number of deleterious effects on the ecology of an estuary. These include a reduction in the populations of the bait species, the death of other, non-target invertebrates, disturbance to feeding waders and wildfowl and the release of pollutants buried in the sediment.

Intensive bait-digging in some parts of Britain, particularly North-East England, has been shown to cause a severe reduction in the populations of both ragworm and lugworm, dug-out areas in some cases taking many months to be repopulated to their original density. Despite such high levels of exploitation, local extinction of these species is probably prevented by the relatively low efficiency of digging, as well as recolonisation from populations in the adjacent mudflats.

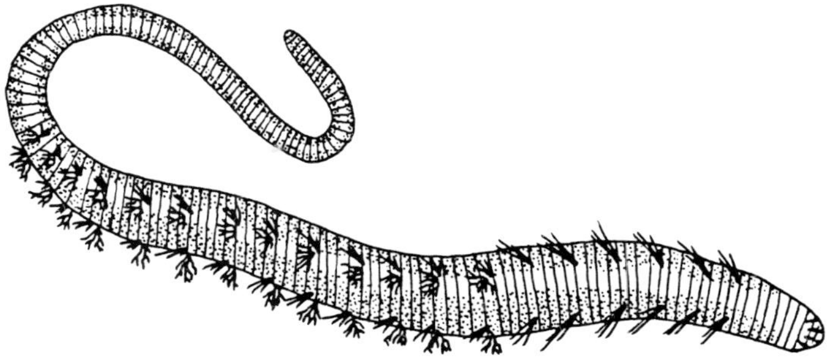

R. C. Dryden

Lugworm.

During digging, sediment is severely disturbed to a depth of about 30 centimetres, and large areas of mudflat may be overturned by one person in a single visit. Clearly there is a high risk of damage to the other invertebrates living within the mud. Some individuals may be buried deep in the sediment, whilst others are trapped on the surface until the next tide, both circumstances often being fatal. Most of the common mud-dwelling species are severely reduced immediately after digging. It has been estimated that for every gram of lugworm harvested, 1.9 grams of other invertebrates are destroyed. Back-filling dug areas may reduce disturbance to other invertebrate species within the sediment. Excessive digging for bait has been suggested as the cause of the decline in the cockle fishery in North Norfolk, and a contributory factor in the case of Southend Flats, Essex. Exposure of the black anoxic layer of the mud during digging can bring large quantities of heavy metals to the surface, which may subsequently enter the food chain and lead to the poisoning of marine life.

In Suffolk there is little commercial exploitation of lug and ragworm populations, bait collection being primarily for private use. Supplies of bait available from angling shops are generally brought in from distant sources such as The Wash, the Essex Mersea and the Continent. Bait-digging in Suffolk is most prevalent during late summer and autumn, and tends to be concentrated in those areas of easiest access, such as Fagbury Flats on the Orwell and Holbrook Bay on the Stour.

The present level of bait-digging in Suffolk is unlikely to cause a significant depletion in the populations of the species concerned. Of greater concern is the potential disturbance to wildlife, especially feeding birds. A large area around each digger, estimated at between 5 and 20 hectares, may be unsuitable for feeding birds, effectively reducing the area of feeding grounds available. Regular human disturbance, whether by bait-diggers or other estuary users, can make areas of the shore more or less permanently unsuitable for some bird species. Food deprivation and the extra energy used when disturbed may result in a higher mortality of birds during periods of adverse weather.

Recently steps have been taken to provide alternative sources of bait for anglers. Two companies, Rebait Limited and Sea Bait Limited, have begun commercial farming of lugworm and ragworm respectively. Farming may well provide a reliable source of high quality bait, with the added advantage of reducing the dependence on natural populations.

Wildfowling and Puntgunning

Wildfowling and puntgunning have been a tradition on the Suffolk estuaries for many decades and until the 1940s provided both income and a valuable source of protein for the local population. Over the last few decades, however, wildfowling in Britain has become solely a recreational pursuit and is enjoyed by over 160,000 people. An estimated 1,000,000 wildfowl are shot and retrieved annually, 70-75% of which are mallard and the remainder mainly wigeon and teal. Studies in the USA suggest that another 20-35% of the number shot are crippled and die unretrieved. Whilst threequarters of the mallard are shot inland, wigeon are primarily shot in coastal regions and the total kill in Britain, including losses from wounded birds, is thought to amount to 60,000-120,000 annually. The peak population of over-wintering wigeon in Britain is 224,000 (average mid-winter peak between 1981-86). The total number shot per year is therefore a significant

T. J. Holzer

percentage of the British population, and as such requires careful management.

On the Suffolk coast wildfowling occurs primarily on the foreshore of estuaries (between the high and low water mark) on land that is owned, with a few exceptions, by the Crown. The British Association for Shooting and Conservation (BASC) has an agreement with the Crown Estate Commissioners enabling their members to legally carry firearms and shoot quarry species on all foreshore owned by the Crown, subject to the restrictions laid down in the Wildlife and Countryside Act 1981. On private foreshore, for instance the Orwell, which is owned by Ipswich Borough Council, and small sections of the Stour, Blyth and Ore, shooting rights are held by the respective owners.

To regulate and manage shooting on our estuaries many wildfowlers have formed clubs affiliated to the BASC, and have negotiated sole shooting rights for selected areas of foreshore. There are now approximately two hundred BASC affiliated coastal clubs in Britain, shooting 74,500 hectares of coastland in England. Such clubs effectively regulate wildfowling by limiting the number of guns (and so preventing over-shooting), improving the shooting standards of members, and controlling illegal and indiscriminate shooting by "marsh cowboys". Clubs, under the guidance of the BASC, are also encouraged to formulate management plans for the area under their tenure. These may provide for the establishment of refuge areas, in which shooting is not allowed, and for the monitoring of bag sizes.

Four wildfowling clubs represent the majority of shooting on the Suffolk estuaries (see table 6). The areas shot by the Alde, Orwell and Stour clubs are all within SSSI's, whilst the other clubs shoot over land that is not protected under the Wildlife and Countryside Act. Wildfowlers who are not members of the above clubs can of course shoot other areas, either under the blanket agreement between

Table 6. Wildfowl Clubs on the Suffolk Estuaries

Club	Site/s	Owner of foreshore	Membership limit	Management plan
Anglian Wildfowlers Association and Gun Club	Stour, Holbrook Bay	Crown	150	None
	Deben, south of Martlesham Creek	Private		None
Grove Shooting Club	Stour, Seafields Bay	Crown	No limit, currently 20 members	Implemented 1987
Leiston and District Wildfowlers Association	Alde, North Shore adjacent to Snape Warren and Blackheath.	Crown	50	Implemented 1988
River Orwell Shooting and Conservation Club	Orwell, north shore and south shore saltmarsh	Ipswich Borough Council	50	None

the BASC and Crown Estate Commissioners (provided they are members of the BASC) or with permission from private landowners who hold the shooting rights over areas of foreshore.

Shooting duck from a purpose-built punt with a large bore fixed shotgun has been practised in Suffolk for many decades. Until the second World War a number of puntguns were used by fishermen, especially on the Alde and Stour, to supplement their income during slack fishing periods. Today puntgunners operate on the Stour (3), Deben (2), Alde (2), Ore (1) and Butley Creek (1). It is impossible to determine the number of duck (primarily wigeon and mallard) that are shot or injured, since no co-ordinated monitoring takes place. It is possible for one shot to kill up to 80 birds (as reported on the Alde in the 1930s), although the average kill is more likely to be between six and ten birds per shot. How often puntgunning occurs is unknown.

Wildfowlers punt (gun removed) on the Stour.

Direct mortality from shooting or the delayed death of crippled birds is not the only impact of wildfowling and puntgunning. Wildfowl seeking grit to aid digestion have been found to ingest discharged lead shot, causing a number of adverse physiological effects. These include muscular paralysis (especially in the gut), damage to the nervous system, kidneys and liver, and anaemia, leading in many cases to death. In the USA lead poisoning from gun shot has caused serious problems and has led to many states banning the use of lead cartridges. Conflicting research in Britain has led the RSPB, Wildfowl Trust and BASC to conclude that lead shot poisoning (from cartridges) is not at present an acute problem, but any deaths are unnecessary if alternatives can be found. The ingestion of pellets in wildfowl varies according to locality, the extent of shooting and the time of year. It is estimated that 2.3% of the British population of mallard die each winter as a direct result of lead shot ingestion, whilst sub-lethal intoxication may impair reproductive ability in many others. In the south coast harbours, up to 12.5% of mallard contain ingested lead pellets, compared with the national average of 4.6%.

In the USA the substitution of non-toxic soft steel for lead shot has provided an effective solution to the problem of lead poisoning. Soft steel, however, can cause barrel damage and is not recommended for some thin-walled guns. The provision of grit, especially in areas where it is scarce, can reduce the ingestion of lead pellets and if calcium is added can also reduce the absorption of lead into the body.

There is circumstantial evidence to suggest that disturbance from shooting affects the distribution and behaviour of waders and wildfowl. Due to the relatively enclosed nature of estuaries disturbance, rather than bird mortality, may be the major problem associated with wildfowling. The BASC and the Wildfowl Trust have jointly funded a project to assess the impact of shooting disturbance. Whilst none of the Suffolk estuaries are planned to be study areas, Hamford Water in Essex is one of the twenty three sites selected for detailed study and may reveal movements between the Stour and Hamford Water related to shooting disturbance. It has been suggested that the issueing of licences to shoot brent geese in Essex may have been the cause of the increased numbers in Suffolk, where only one licence has been issued.

Shellfisheries

Large scale commercial exploitation of shellfish only occurs in a few areas around Britain. The species collected include mussels, cockles, and oysters (including our native oyster and the introduced pacific and portuguese oysters).

A. W. Boyle

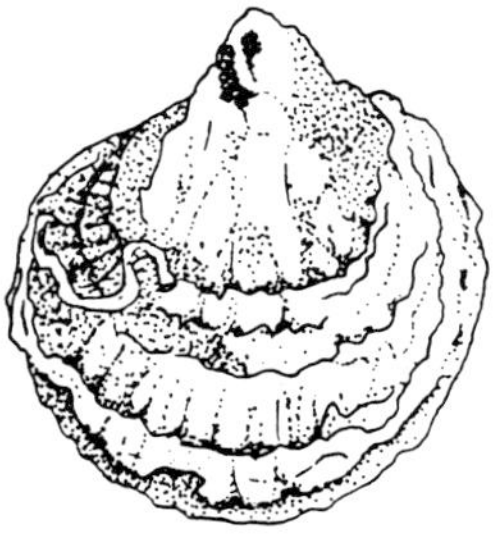

Native oyster.

Portuguese oyster

Shellfish may be farmed in structures built on the intertidal mudflats, or harvested directly from the intertidal sediment (bottom culture). Shellfisheries are regulated by the Ministry for Agriculture, Fisheries and Food, who issue Several Orders granting permission to culture shellfish. Farming on intertidal areas also requires a lease from the owners of the foreshore, who are invariably the Crown.

Shellfish harvested for human consumption require clean water, and the EEC has set water quality criteria for farmed areas under the Shellfish Waters Directive (79/923/EEC). Under the Directive member states designate shellfish waters where the water quality is supposedly improved or protected to within the set limits. The UK has so far designated twenty-nine shellfish waters (all of which already fulfilled the criteria before designation or required no alterations to improvements already planned), one of which is Butley Creek.

Exploitation of shellfish in the Suffolk estuaries was once an important part of the local economy. In medieval days regulations on the Orwell limited the months in which dredging for oysters could proceed in beds at Shotley, Collimer Point and Nacton. There are also records of oyster beds on the Stour, Ore and Alde. In 1650 a water bailiff was employed to control the beds on the Ore to check that no undersized oysters were harvested. Today the wild oyster no longer inhabits the Orwell or the Stour and has not been recorded on the Alde/Ore/Butley, Deben or Blyth. The only remaining oyster farm exists in Butley Creek where the Butley Oysterage farm portuguese oysters. Two other Several Orders have been issued by MAFF, one on the Deben and another on the Blyth. Neither are in operation today, but there is a possibility of mussel farming starting in Stonyditch Creek on Orfordness.

Disused oyster bed on the Ore.

Shellfish operations on the Suffolk estuaries today are environmentally benign and may even ensure that water quality is maintained. There is however, likely to be an increase in the number of shellfish operations over the next few years as the European and British market expands. This may well involve new techniques and species for cultivation, some of which are the cause of much concern in other regions of the country. Extensive new operations covering large areas of mudflat would cause substantial disturbance to feeding waders, and the escape of introduced alien species may unbalance the local ecology.

For many centuries oysters were gathered on the Ore by dragging with a scrope-net and whilst oysters are no longer harvested in this manner, commercial cockle harvesting is achieved by dredging. One of the major cockle fisheries in Britain is in the Outer Thames and on a few occasions dredgers have moved out of this area and into the Orwell and Stour. The cockle dredger scoops up the top several centimetres of sediment to a width of 0.6 metres in each trawl, and has greatly increased the area fished and number of cockles harvested. The effects of continuous delivery hydraulic dredging on the invertebrate fauna within the sediment is unclear and under researched.

Cockle dredger.

Saltmarsh Erosion

Saltmarsh erosion occurs whenever tidal conditions change such that there is a net removal of sediment from the salt marsh. The consequent lowering of the marsh surface results in a reversal of the successional changes characteristic of saltmarsh formation, so that the middle marsh reverts to low marsh or bare mudflat. Erosion may lead to undercutting of the marsh surface with resultant slumping, leaving behind a vertical saltmarsh "cliff" that can be over one metre in height. Further erosion leads to the gradual retreat of the saltmarsh landwards.

Many of the saltmarshes bordering the Suffolk estuaries, and particularly those which are nearest the open sea (and so more exposed), are currently being eroded. Substantial saltmarsh cliffs occur in a number of areas including Shotley and Levington on the Orwell and the lower reaches of the Ore and Deben estuaries. In Copperas Bay on the Stour the saltmarsh cliff retreated at a rate of 3 centimetres per month over a nine month period in 1975/6. The absolute seaward limit of saltmarsh vegetation decreased by 3 metres over a two and a half year period, and the surface level of the marsh fell by 2 centimetres in 17 months. More recently 50 metres of saltmarsh are estimated to have eroded from Erwarton Bay on the opposite side of the estuary, in the last fifteen years. In contrast there are relatively few areas of saltmarsh accretion and those that occur are in the more sheltered parts of the estuaries, for example north of Waldringfield on the Deben and around Iken on the Alde.

Although cycles of accretion and erosion are a normal feature of saltmarsh development, it is probable that the recent losses of marsh in Suffolk are part of an underlying trend in the direction of erosion. The large difference in surface height between the saltmarsh flat and the adjacent mudflat suggests that a great deal of sediment accretion would be required before any increase in the area of marsh could occur. Erosion of Suffolk saltmarshes may mirror changes in other parts of East Anglia, for example the Dengie Peninsular in Essex, where 10% of the saltmarsh was lost between 1960 and 1981.

The observed losses in saltmarsh may be related to the sinking of the land surface of South-East England. The current rate of sinking is believed to be about 3 millimetres per year. Sediment accretion must equal this rate if the height of the marsh with respect to sea level is to remain constant. If accretion is less than the rate of sinking, then saltmarsh erosion will result. It is possible that over an extended timespan saltmarsh erosion and accretion may correspond to periods of rapid sinking and stasis of the land surface.

An alternative explanation for the loss of saltmarsh is that their exposure has changed. Formerly many saltmarshes were fronted by large beds of eel-grass but in the 1930s most of these beds were destroyed by an epidemic of "wasting disease". The removal of the protection given by this vegetation may have resulted in the erosion of mudflats and saltmarsh. A similar increase in erosion may exist in *Spartina anglica* dominated communities in which "die-back" has occurred (see chapter 2). Saltmarsh erosion may also be accelerated by the wash from commercial shipping and pleasure craft.

Apart from the loss of an important wildlife habitat, saltmarsh erosion may have serious economic implications. Saltmarshes are often an integral component of coastal defences, reducing the height and dissipating the energy of waves before they reach the seawall. The cost of building an unprotected concrete seawall (over a million pounds per kilometre) is twenty times that of a stone capped earth embankment fronted by saltmarsh. Consequently there are strong financial as well as environmental reasons for the protection and conservation of saltmarshes.

Chapter 4 The Future

Introduction

In previous chapter the impact of many activities on the Suffolk estuaries has been discussed. It is clear that a number of these are changing the ecology of our estuaries in a fashion that is neither sustainable nor in some instances necessary.

In this final chapter two sets of recommendations are presented. Firstly, topics deserving further research are outlined. Secondly, a number of management suggestions are put forward which may help to mitigate and monitor the impact of many activities on wildlife.

Essential Research

In reviewing past information on the wildlife of the Suffolk estuaries, it is clear that there has been an emphasis on ornithological surveys. Other aspects of the ecosystem tend to be less attractive and harder to study. Nevertheless, other areas of research are essential in order to understand the basic ecology of our estuaries and detect any fluctuations resulting from either natural or human influences.

INVERTEBRATE RESEARCH

Monitoring the invertebrate fauna of the Orwell and Stour has revealed some interesting, and as yet unexplained, changes over the last fifteen years. These studies need to be extended to the other estuaries and the causes of fluctuations investigated in greater detail.

ORNITHOLOGICAL RESEARCH

The BOEE counts of roosting waders and wildfowl have provided invaluable information on the importance of Suffolk for over-wintering and passage shore-birds. Feeding counts have provided more detail on how waders and wildfowl utilise the intertidal mudflats. This information is vital in order to respond to the threat of future developments, facilitating an accurate assessment of the environmental impact of any proposals.

Further studies to monitor the distribution of feeding waders and wildfowl on all of the estuaries are essential. In addition detailed analysis of the changes in distribution of waders on the Orwell are of specific interest, as Fagbury is destroyed by the construction of the Felixstowe Dock extension.

The importance of the Suffolk estuaries for breeding waders will be ascertained once the current SWT survey is complete. Careful monitoring of these populations will be required in the future.

BOTANICAL RESEARCH

The erosion of mudflats on the Stour and Orwell is clearly a problem. The communities of eel-grass and algae inhabiting the mud surface play an important role in controlling the extent of erosion on both the mudflat and adjacent saltmarsh. Careful monitoring of these communities, and the factors which influence their establishment and growth, is essential in order to understand and limit further erosion.

Current research into the effects of heavy metals, TBT and other pollutants, on the growth of intertidal plant communities needs careful studying and the implications acted upon by the relevant local organisations.

SALTMARSH EROSION

The exact extent of saltmarsh erosion in Suffolk is unknown. A comprehensive study is required to review the areas involved and investigate the causes in detail. Saltmarsh is important in protecting sea walls (see chapter 3) and is therefore of considerable economic value. In Essex, Anglian Water have instigated a large project to prevent erosion and promote accretion of saltmarsh, using faggots and small fields of plastic mesh fencing on areas of intertidal mudflat fronting saltmarshes. If successful, these techniques could be extended to protect saltmarsh in Suffolk.

The possible causes of erosion have been discussed elsewhere (chapter 2 and 3), but also require nationally co-ordinated research. The degree to which wash from ships promotes saltmarsh erosion, particularly on the Orwell and Stour, requires further attention. Enforcement of speed limits may help reduce wash-induced erosion.

GRAZING

The influence of grazing on saltmarsh communities is well documented. Overgrazing causes poaching and the loss of vegetation, promoting erosion. In Suffolk only small areas of saltmarsh are grazed and care needs to be taken to avoid overgrazing. A review of the areas and condition of grazed saltmarsh is necessary.

The intensity of grazing can have a strong influence on the suitability of an area of saltmarsh for breeding waders. There is therefore an opportunity to improve many areas of saltmarsh for breeding waders by the manipulation of grazing pressure.

The effect of grazing on saltmarsh vegetation. Overgrazed marsh to left of fence, ungrazed marsh to right.

VISITOR PRESSURE

The impact of recreational activities, particularly on shingle vegetation, requires further research. The identification of sensitive sites will enable appropriate management to be implemented, and so mitigate any detrimental effects.

Management suggestions for the long term conservation of the Suffolk estuaries.

SEWAGE AND OTHER ORGANIC EFFLUENTS

The discharge of organic effluents into our estuaries requires strict management. Anglian Water are particularly concerned about the upper reaches of the Orwell and have recently completed a mathematical model to predict the changes that are necessary to improve water quality. Despite some recent improvements, due to many industries leaving the dock area or improving their discharges, the Orwell is still a class 4 polluted river. Clearly there is a need for further improvements to both the industrial and domestic discharges. It has to be noted that a limited amount of nutrient enrichment enhances the biological productivity of mudflats, but improvements are clearly necessary to bring the upper reaches of the Orwell in line with acceptable water quality standards.

Biological monitoring of the intertidal mudflats by Anglian Water is essential and surveys of the invertebrate fauna of the Orwell and Stour need to be undertaken on a regular basis. The results of the ITE and SWT surveys clearly indicate changes in the invertebrate fauna which require further investigation. Biological monitoring would identify trends in the abundance and distribution of invertebrates and provide an indication of the ecological health of the system.

HEAVY METAL AND TBT POLLUTION

Environmental Quality Standards for mercury and cadmium are set by EEC Directives on discharges, and other heavy metals are controlled by proposed Water Quality Standards. There is often insufficient data on the effects of heavy metals on marine organisms. The proposed Water Quality Standards for estuaries in Britain are in some cases inadequate, and are often higher than concentrations already known to have adverse effects on many species. The situation clearly requires further nationally coordinated research.

The impact of TBT on the invertebrate fauna of the Suffolk estuaries is unknown. Whether the ban on retail sale of certain anti-fouling paints containing TBT will solve the problems identified in other estuaries remains to be seen. Clearly the input of TBT from ships using Felixstowe, Harwich, and in particular Ipswich, requires further investigation and may well be having an impact on the fauna of the Orwell and Stour.

Ipswich Dock.

Adherence to the guidelines for applying and removing anti-fouling paint, set out by the Department of the Environment, should be monitored in marinas and docks on the estuaries. Regular surveillance of TBT levels in the sediment, water and invertebrates in the mudflats adjacent to docks and marinas would highlight the effectiveness of each boatyard in complying with the guidelines and is clearly essential if further pollution is to be prevented.

OIL POLLUTION

The inherent problems associated with transporting, loading and unloading oil products in enclosed water systems (chapter 3) require strict management. Difficulties associated with navigation, and in particular the likelihood of collisions, must be eliminated. This may require a tighter control of, or perhaps a reduction in, the number of moorings congesting the navigable channel. Improvements in safety procedures and the use of pilots, or a reduction in the number and size of ships carrying potentially lethal products would also lessen the chances of collision. The position of Ipswich at the head of a relatively thin and shallow estuary make this Port very unsuitable for handling many modern and dangerous cargoes. The need for strict safety procedures is therefore of paramount importance.

Quay activities also require improvements. The release of any chemical that kills swans and gulls (chapter 3) is clearly unacceptable and the effects these discharges are having on other estuarine fauna is as yet completely unresearched and unknown. Loading and unloading potential pollutants, and the procedures for cleaning contaminated machinery and surfaces, need to be designed such that pollution of the water cannot occur.

Improvements clearly need the cooperation of the Navigation Authorities, who under the Oil Pollution Act (1971) are responsible for oil pollution, Anglian Water who are responsible for water quality, and the relevant industries to identify and eliminate potential pollution risks.

CHANNEL DREDGING

The full impacts of dredging have not been properly assessed. It is surely the responsibilty of the Ipswich Port Authority and Harwich Harbour Board, both of which carry out dredging, to initiate detailed studies to assess the wider environmental implications of all past, present and future dredging operations. The information in this report clearly suggests that channel dredging and straightening may have caused substantial erosion of mudflats and saltmarshes, and corresponding changes in the fauna and flora. Future dredging activities should be limited to a level which does not further accentuate erosion.

BAITDIGGING

The severe problems associated with baitdigging in other areas of Britain have not yet been experienced in Suffolk. Nevertheless, the impact of digging on invertebrate populations, and the disturbance to feeding waders and wildfowl, should be monitored. A system of licencing for local diggers (especially in the most sensitive areas) may keep the extent of digging within acceptable limits, but would require both wardening and administrative time in order to be successful.

Babergh District Council have expressed an interest in designating parts of the Orwell and Stour as Local Nature Reserves, which would enable them to introduce bye-laws to control baitdigging.

The recent establishment of both lug and ragworm farms in Britain may help reduce the threat of future large-scale commercial baitdigging in Suffolk.

WILDFOWLING AND PUNTGUNNING

The formation of wildfowling clubs has proved to be a successful mechanism for controlling and managing shooting on our estuaries. The initiation of further clubs should be encouraged, together with the compilation of management plans. It is apparent that wildfowling can have a significant local impact on the populations of certain quarry species. However, details of the numbers of duck shot are not collected and are essential in order to properly assess, monitor and manage quarry species over-wintering in Suffolk. Refuge areas, designated in the wildfowling management plans, require careful selection and cooperation between the clubs and the BTO, RSPB, NCC and SWT is essential to identify the most suitable areas. Monitoring of wildfowl populations, together with quarry statistics, may highlight the need for voluntary shooting restrictions on selected species.

The large proportion of birds crippled during puntgunning is completely unacceptable. This activity is no longer a way of life or an essential source of income and in the view of the SWT should be banned on the Suffolk estuaries.

RECLAMATION

Further loss of the intertidal zone, due to industrial or recreational development, is incompatible with conservation of both the wildlife and landscape interest of the Suffolk estuaries. The County Structure Plan outlines strict planning policies with regard to further developments within the Heritage Coast, the Suffolk Coast and Heaths AONB and the coastal SSSI's. Adherence to these policies is essential to prevent damaging developments and the loss of further intertidal habitat.

RECREATION

The detrimental impact of recreational pressure can be alleviated by careful forward planning. The implemention of management plans for sensitive and/or valuable sites has helped promote and conserve many important features of landscape and wildlife interest on the Suffolk coast. Both the Heritage Coast Project, run by the County Council, and the Shotley Peninsula Project, run by Babergh District Council, are successful examples of such plans. A River Orwell North Shore Management Plan will be implemented towards the end of 1988 and will manage the increased pressure that this area will experience as Ipswich expands.

SHELLFISHERIES

There are currently no problems associated with shellfish harvesting in Suffolk, although two activities, hydraulic cockle dredging and the cultivation of alien species, may pose threats in the future. Cockle dredging causes severe disturbance to the invertebrate populations of both intertidal and subtidal sediments, the impact of which is unknown. Research into this activity is currently underway and until this is completed it is hoped that cockle dredging will not be allowed in Suffolk, especially on those mudflats that lie within Sites of Special Scientific Interest.

The farming of alien species of shellfish, for instance the manilla clam, may pose a threat to the ecology of intertidal mudflats (chapter 3). Should such operations be proposed for Suffolk it is hoped that environmental considerations will outweigh those of commerce.

Marsh harrier.

Practical Management

There are a number of management practices that could improve the wildlife interest of the estuaries. The success of the RSPB reserve at Havergate Island has demonstrated how grazing marsh can be converted to brackish lagoons, creating exceptional habitats for breeding waders, wildfowl and terns. Many other sites could be developed along similar lines. The Suffolk Wildlife Trust, for instance, has recently taken on the management of a mud-settling lagoon at Levington on the north shore of the Orwell.

Eighty-four hectares of Trimley Marshes, adjacent to Fagbury, are soon to be developed into a nature reserve as compensation for the loss of Fagbury mudflats and saltmarsh caused by the Felixstowe Dock extension. Although this reserve is no substitute for the loss of the intertidal zone, the development of brackish and freshwater lagoons surrounded by reedbeds and grazing marsh will create a valuable nature reserve.

It is hoped that the establishment of the Suffolk River Valleys ESA will increase the area of grassland suitable for breeding waders. The results of the 1988 SWT breeding wader survey will identify the most important areas of saltmarsh and grazing marsh in Suffolk. The study will also highlight those sites that would benefit most from small changes in management practices, for instance a short delay in rolling or cutting in spring, preventing the destruction of nests. Many of these sites would be protected and improved if entered into an ESA agreement with MAFF.

The best form of protection is perhaps the arrangment of management agreements with landowners or setting up of nature reserves, where valuable areas can be carefully managed, studied and protected. With the information gathered by the Estuaries Project it is hoped that the most valuable sites will be identified and their long term protection and management secured.

Conclusion

It is apparent from the information contained in this report that most activities have an impact on the ecology of the estuaries, and that many are detrimental to the long term conservation of the system. Safeguarding the important species and communities that inhabit the Suffolk estuaries requires the conservation and sensitive management of the whole ecosystem. In order to harmonise the conflicts that exist, it is clear that each user group must become more accountable for their activities. This requires cooperation and coordination between the various user groups and interested parties, and a deeper understanding of the wider impact of each operation. The formation of a users association for each estuary, and particularly for the Orwell and Stour, which are subject to the greatest pressures, would help secure the future of their wildlife.

Appendix

Index of Scientific Names

Birds

Black-Throated Diver	Gavia arctica
Great Northern Diver	Gavia immer
Little Grebe	Tachybaptus ruficollis
Great Crested Grebe	Podiceps cristatus
Red-Necked Grebe	Podiceps griseigena
Slavonian Grebe	Podiceps auritus
Cormorant	Phalacrocorax carbo
Grey Heron	Ardea cinerea
Mute Swan	Cygnus olor
Bewick's Swan	Cygnus columbianus
Whooper Swan	Cygnus cygnus
Bean Goose	Anser fabalis
White-Fronted Goose	Anser albifrons
Greylag Goose	Anser anser
Canada Goose	Branta canadensis
Barnacle Goose	Branta leucopsis
Brent Goose	Branta bernicia
Red-Breasted Goose	Branta ruficollis
Shelduck	Tadorna tadorna
Wigeon	Anas penelope
Gadwall	Anas strepera
Teal	Anas crecca
Mallard	Anas platyrhynchos
Pintail	Anas acuta
Shoveler	Anas clypeata
Pochard	Aythya ferina
Tufted Duck	Aythya fuligula
Scaup	Aythya marila
Eider	Somateria mollissima
Long-Tailed Duck	Clangula hyemalis
Common Scoter	Melanitta nigra
Velvet Scoter	Melanitta fusca
Goldeneye	Bucephala clangula
Smew	Mergus albellus
Red-Breasted Merganser	Mergus serrator
Goosander	Mergus merganser
Oystercatcher	Haematopus ostralegus
Avocet	Recurvirostra avosetta
Ringed Plover	Charadrius hiaticula
Golden Plover	Pluvialis apricaria
Grey Plover	Pluvialis squatarola

Lapwing	Vanellus vanellus
Knot	Calidris canutus
Sanderling	Calidris alba
Dunlin	Calidris alpina
Ruff	Philomachus pugnax
Jack Snipe	Lymnocryptes minimus
Snipe	Gallinago gallinago
Black-Tailed Godwit	Limosa limosa
Bar-Tailed Godwit	Limosa lapponica
Whimbrel	Numenius phaeopus
Curlew	Numenius arquata
Spotted Redshank	Tringa erythropus
Redshank	Tringa totanus
Greenshank	Tringa nebularia
Green Sandpiper	Tringa ochropus
Common Sandpiper	Actitis hypoleucos
Turnstone	Arenaria interpres
Black-Headed Gull	Larus ridibundus
Common Gull	Larus canus
Lesser Black-Backed Gull	Larus fuscus
Herring Gull	Larus argentatus
Glaucous Gull	Larus hyperboreus
Great Black-Backed Gull	Larus marinus
Little Tern	Sterna albifrons
Skylark	Alauda arvensis
Meadow Pipit	Anthus pratensis

Plants

Annual Sea-Blight	Suaeda maritima
Common Eel-grass	Zostera marina
Dwarf Eel-grass	Zostera noltii
English Cord-grass	Spartina anglica
Glasswort	Salicornia europaea
Golden Samphire	Inula crithmoides
Lax-flowered Sea Lavender	Limonium humile
Narrow-Leaved Eel-grass	Zostera angustifolia
Rock Sea Lavender	Limonium binervosum
Saltmarsh Grass	Puccinellia maritima
Sea Arrow-grass	Triglochin maritima
Sea Aster	Aster tripolium
Sea Beet	Beta maritima
Sea Couch	Elymus pungens
Sea Kale	Crambe maritima
Sea Heath	Frankenia laevis
Sea Holly	Eryngium maritimum
Sea Lavender	Limonium vulgare

Sea Pea	Lathyrus japonicus
Sea Plantain	Plantago maritima
Sea Purslane	Halimione portulacoides
Sea Spurge	Euphorbia paralias
Stinking Goosefoot	Chenopodium vulvaria
Thrift	Armeria maritima
Yellow-Horned Poppy	Glaucium flavum
Yellow Vetch	Vicia lutea

Fish

Bass	Dicentrarchus labrax
Cod	Gadus morhua
Common Eel	Anguilla anguilla
Flounder	Platichthys flesus
Herring	Clupea harengus
Plaice	Pleuronectes platessa
Salmon	Salmo salar
Sand Smelt	Atherina presbyter
Sea Trout	Salmo trutta
Sole	Solea solea
Whiting	Merlangius merlangus

Molluscs

Baltic Tellin	Macoma balthica
Common Cockle	Cerastoderma edule
Common Oyster	Ostrea edulis
Common Mussel	Mytilus edulis
Dogwhelk	Nucella lapillus
Pacific Oyster	Crassostrea
Portuguese Oyster	Crassostrea angulata
Sand Gaper	Mya arenaria

Annelids

Lugworm	Arenicola marina
Ragworm	Nereis diversicolor

Arthropods

Common Shore Crab	Carcinus maenas

Further Reading

Arnott, W. G. (1952). Alde Estuary. Norman Adlard, Ipswich.
Arnott, W. G. (1954). Suffolk Estuary. Norman Adlard, Ipswich.
Arnott, W. G. (1954). Orwell Estuary. Norman Adlard, Ipswich.
Barnes, R. S. K. (1974). Estuarine Biology. Edward Arnold, London.
Barnes, R. S. K. (1977). The Coastline. Wiley, London.
Barrett, J. and Yonge, C. M. (1958). Collins Pocket Guide to the Sea Shore. Collins, London.
Boorman, L. A. and Ranwell, D. S. (1977). Ecology of Maplin Sands and the Coastal Zones of Suffolk, Essex and North Kent. Institute of Terrestial Ecology, Cambridge.
Campbell, A. C. (1976). The Hamlyn Guide to the Seashore and Shallow Seas of Britain and Europe. Hamlyn, London.
Clark, R. B. (1986). Marine Pollution. Clarendon Press. Oxford.
Long, S. P. and Mason, C. F. (1983). Saltmarsh Ecology. Blackie, Glasgow.
McLusky, D. S. (1981). The Estuarine Ecosystem. Blackie, Glasgow.
North Sea Forum (1987). The Report of the North Sea Forum.
Owen, M., Atkinson-Willies, G. L. and Salmon, D. G. (1986). Wildfowl in Great Britain. The University Press, Cambridge.
Parker, R. (1978). Men of Dunwich. Collins, London.
Prater, A. J. (1981). Estuary Birds of Britain and Ireland. Poyser, Calton.
Ranwell, D. S. (1972). Ecology of Salt Marshes and Sand Dunes. Chapman and Hall, London.

A detailed bibliography of publications relating to the Suffolk estuaries is available from the Suffolk Wildlife Trust.